The Christian Family Prepares for Christmas

DAILY DEVOTIONS FOR THE ADVENT SEASON

by CHARLES S. MUELLER

special projects by DIANE DIETERICH

pencil sketches by MARY BETH GAITSKILL

CONCORDIA PUBLISHING HOUSE · ST. LOUIS, MISSOURI

Concordia Publishing House, St. Louis, Missouri
Concordia Publishing House Ltd., London, W. C. 1
© 1965 by Concordia Publishing House
MANUFACTURED IN THE UNITED STATES OF AMERICA

Since the early days of the church, God's people have prepared for a proper celebration of Christmas. They have established a season of the church year, Advent, for this particular reason. Advent begins on the fourth Sunday before Christmas and ends on Christmas Eve. During the Advent season Christians get ready on every level of life for a God-pleasing remembrance and celebration of the great day on which the Savior was born.

Preface

It *was* a great day. On it for a moment God tore open the heavens and let the angelic ecstasy break down on the ears of men. It was the day that marked the beginning of the end for Satan and his power and set the Light of the world firmly in the midst of sin's inky blackness. It was a day eagerly anticipated by the prophets of old and joyfully remembered by His people of the New Age.

This devotional guide was prepared to help you in your preparation. It was prepared for families — whole families. While any Christian may use it, the author had in mind the family unit, mother, father, and children, gathered around the dining room table or simply sitting in a circle as they talk with one another and with God about the wonder of Christmas. It is written so that Christian could speak with Christian and no one, regardless of age, be overlooked in this faith-building interchange of witness and instruction. Use it that way. It will not be easy, for such Christian conversation is not common. It is difficult and very rare. Put effort into the preparation of each devotion, and each devotion will help you prepare for the finest Christmas you have ever experienced.

This book follows a seven-day devotional plan. Each day is different and has a different emphasis.

> Sunday — A Preparation Hymn
> Monday — God Prepares for Man
> Tuesday — Open-End Preparation Story
> Wednesday — Man Prepares to Serve God
> Thursday — A Preparation Project
> Friday — A Preparation Word
> Saturday — A Preparation Psalm

You may wish to use the following order for your devotional service.

> In the name of the Father and of the Son and of the Holy Ghost. Amen.
>
> Scripture Text for the Day
>
> Devotional Meditation
>
> Family Discussion

Advent Hymn of the Week

Prayer and Lord's Prayer

Thursday evening is especially different. That evening the entire family will want to spend at least an hour together. During this hour a devotional device can be made. It is designed so that everyone can participate to a degree. If you try this approach to preparation and purposeful joint activity, you will reap benefits in both your private devotional life and your family life together. Specific directions for the construction of this device may be found on pages 41—59.

You may wish to use the devotions in a different order. Do it. You may wish to experiment with a variety of approaches. Do it. This is Advent. You are preparing. You are helping others prepare. Anything that will accomplish the goals is acceptable.

May God bless you with His presence during this Advent and give you a Christ-filled Christmas.

I wish to acknowledge the work of Diane Dieterich, who developed the projects, and the cooperation of the people of St. Andrew, who first used these devotions in family preparation for Christmas.

The evangelist John frequently talked about Christ as the Light of the world. This name was not new to him. Isaiah, many years before, looking ahead to our world, said, "The people that walked in darkness have seen a great light."

The Advent Wreath

BEFORE ADVENT BEGINS
John 1:4, 5

Christmas is all about this Light of the world. Advent reminds us that there is still much darkness. It is a darkness made up of sin, ignorance, hate, and pride. To remind themselves of the growing power of Christ, the Light, Christians have long made and used Advent wreaths.

The wreath is covered with evergreen. Just as this particular species of tree is always green, so our hope for eternity is always sure because it is based on Christ. Green is the color of life and growth. Around our wreath we will pray God to bring us closer to Him and help us stay alive and grow in faith and hope.

The wreath is also in the form of a circle. A circle has no beginning and no end. What better way to picture eternity to our minds than this? Our life with God is everlasting, beginning, always, now.

The candles are significant both in their color and in their light. The four candles on the edge of the wreath are violet. Violet is the color of repentance. During the next four weeks we want to look inward and see ourselves as the sinners we are. *

The first candle is lighted before the devotions on the First Sunday in Advent. During this first week only the one candle glows when we worship. On each succeeding Sunday, as we draw nearer to Christ's birthday, another candle is lit until finally all are aflame.

The light these candles put forth may be small, but these flames, growing brighter each week, stress the growing power of Christ Jesus over darkness. On Christmas Eve the candle within the circle is lighted. This is the Christ Child candle, telling us that He who is the Light for our darkness has been born.

When we have made our wreath, let us join hands and ask God for strength as we use this worship aid, and pray that we may use it to glorify Him.

Instructions: The Advent wreath is basically a ring in which are placed five candles. An excellent wreath may be made of a plastic-foam ring about 12 inches in diameter. The size may vary according to taste. Into this ring insert four violet candles equally spaced. If such candles are not to be found, tie a bit of purple ribbon around each candle. Some people place a larger candle in the middle. It is called the Christ Child candle. Still others place a cross or a small crèche in the center. Attach to the ring pine twigs and cones, holly leaves and berries, and other types of evergreen leaves. The circle may also be made of wire, the lid of a basket, or wood.

*(See Cover) A rose-colored candle may be used for the third Sunday, which is called joyful Sunday.

Philip Doddridge, the author of the hymn "Hark the Glad Sound! The Savior Comes," was born the last of 20 children. Of the 20 children only he and a sister lived through childhood. His parents died when he was 13. On his own he got an education and at the age of 28 became a minister. Life was certainly not easy for him. Before he reached the late teens, he faced many tragedies. Thinking of this it is surprising he could write such a beautiful and happy song, "Hark the Glad Sound! The Savior Comes."

"Hark the Glad Sound! The Savior Comes"

FIRST WEEK IN ADVENT
Sunday
Luke 4:18;
Isaiah 61:1, 2

A Preparation Hymn

He wrote this hymn while preparing a sermon based on Luke 4:18 and Isaiah 61:1, 2. These are the words Christ used for His first sermon. Pastor Doddridge felt so inspired that he quickly wrote this hymn and had the congregation sing it after his sermon on December 28, 1735. Imagine how many millions of times one or more of God's people have sung this thrilling song since then!

But what is the hymn about? Let us read each stanza aloud and then discuss it.

1. Hark the glad sound! The Savior comes,
   The Savior promised long;
   Let every heart prepare a throne
   And every voice a song.

What does this stanza say?

2. He comes the prisoners to release,
   In Satan's bondage held.
   The gates of brass before Him burst,
   The iron fetters yield.

This is another way of saying, "He hath sent Me to . . . proclaim liberty to the captives and the opening of prison to them that are bound" (Isaiah 61:1). Who are the prisoners? Are there any still in prison?

3. He comes the broken heart to bind,
   The bleeding soul to cure,
   And with the treasures of His grace
   T'enrich the humble poor.

"The treasures of His grace" are mentioned in this stanza. Mention a few. We might begin with God's forgiveness, His love, Baptism, and — are there more?

4. Our glad hosannas, Prince of Peace,
   Thy welcome shall proclaim
   And heaven's eternal arches ring
   With Thy belovèd name.

The first stanza says that we *ought* to welcome Him. How would you describe this last stanza?

Now we are ready to sing this hymn. Sing it with Philip Doddridge's joyful anticipation.

(Additional copies of this hymn are found in the back of the book.)

God Prepared the World for Us

FIRST WEEK
IN ADVENT
Monday
Genesis 1:1-27

God Prepared for Man

Our theme of Advent is preparation. We prepare. We prepare for the celebration of Jesus' birth. We can say in a sense that we prepare for the coming of God. But the reverse is also true. God prepared for the coming of man. God tells us about this in the Book of Genesis.

Genesis 1 outlines how the world was made by God. Step by step, layer by layer the picture of creation builds before our very eyes. First came light so that creation could be seen, not by God but by man. God doesn't need light to "see." In rapid succession came the division of the heavens from the earth and of dry land from water. Trees, animals, sun, moon, and stars all had their creative moment. When everything was nearly finished, God spoke those electric words: "Let Us make man." Everything was now ready for the final act. Only the crown of God's creation, the one for whom it had all been called into being, was not yet on the scene. The holy writer tells us, "So God created man in His own image." (Genesis 1:27)

Look at creation through God's eyes. How carefully He prepared everything — for man! Count but a few of the many splendid things He planned and then created to make our life complete. When we have done that, we shall be ready to better reckon with the question, "How shall we prepare for Him?"

Let us talk about it.

"Boy, Mom," said Ricky, "you should have seen it! A man was hanging wreaths on the telephone poles."

"And right above the stoplight, down by the drugstore, he stuck a great big Santa Claus," Mark continued eagerly. "Wow! What a Santa Claus!"

"Looks to me like you boys are getting the Christmas spirit," answered their mother. "So have I. All day long wonderful songs have been playing on the radio. You know the ones. 'I'm Dreaming of a White Christmas' and 'I Saw Mommy Kissing Santa Claus' and a lot of other old favorites. It sounded so nice and Christmasy. I guess we're all catching the Christmas bug."

The Christmas Spirit

FIRST WEEK IN ADVENT
Tuesday

A Preparation Open-End Story

Everyone was excited but Beth. She had been studying in her room. Just before Ricky and Mark came charging in through the back door, she came into the kitchen for a glass of milk.

"Well, I sure haven't got that spirit," said Beth wistfully. "Not yet anyway. I guess I haven't heard enough of the music or seen the decorations. Maybe I'm just different. I remember last year that it wasn't until we started wrapping the presents that suddenly everything took on a kind of glow. I hope this year it comes earlier."

That's the way the conversation continued until Dad came home. As soon as he came through the door, he could tell that everyone was in a good mood. Rick and Mark tumbled over themselves telling him about the man putting up decorations and the size of the Santa at the stoplight.

"I wish we could bottle all this good spirit and keep it till next August," Dad said with a laugh. "Wouldn't that be something?"

Later that night, when the kids were all in bed, Mr. and Mrs. Humes were talking.

"Those boys certainly were excited this afternoon. I guess I was, too. I'm glad we've got the Christmas spirit early," said Mrs. Humes.

"I'm not sure we have," said Mr. Humes, looking up from his paper.

"I don't understand what you mean," answered his wife with a little worried frown.

"Well, I don't think that the real Christmas spirit can be triggered by a couple of evergreen wreaths or by last year's Santa even when he's perched on a stoplight or by the strains of old Christmas melodies. There's something missing when those things stir a feeling which we call the Christmas spirit. The Christmas spirit is something else. I think it's —"

Now let's make a proper ending for this story.

Julie liked church. She liked the singing. She liked the sermon. She liked the prayers. She liked everything about church. But the part she liked the best was when each Sunday the pastor would read the Gospel for the day. It was usually about something Jesus said or did.

Palm Sunday in Advent

FIRST WEEK IN ADVENT
Wednesday
Matthew 21:1-11

Men Who Prepared for God

On this particular Sunday the pastor began by saying, "The Gospel for this, the First Sunday in Advent, is written in the 21st chapter of the Gospel according to St. Matthew, beginning at the first verse." Then he read the Word of God. Julie was all set to hear something read which would remind her of Christmas. She knew that when Advent came, it was only a few weeks until Christmas. She was sure the reading would be Christmasy. But when the pastor read, it wasn't about Christmas at all. If anything, it made her think of Easter, for he was reading the Palm Sunday story.

"What in the world!" thought Julie. "The pastor must have made a mistake. He's reading the wrong thing." No, he wasn't. On the First Sunday in Advent the Gospel is about Jesus' entry into Jerusalem. If she had listened carefully to what the pastor was reading, it wouldn't have been nearly as strange as she thought.

At first hearing all the story tells us about is Christ's triumphant entry into Jerusalem just before His crucifixion. But let us look again. Not only is the Gospel about what Christ did, it also tells us about the actions of other men. It is the story of how a number of men made preparation for His coming.

First there was the man who owned the donkey. He made preparation. Then there were the disciples. They made preparation. Finally there are the many men and women, boys and girls who shouted their hosannas as Jesus went by. They, too, had to prepare. Let us talk about these three different "preparations." How did each get ready?

In a few weeks Christmas will come. On that day we shall join with Christians all over the world in thanking God for the gift of a Savior. We shall sing the songs sung by Christians for hundreds of years. We shall read the very Scripture lessons heard by God's children who lived 2,000 years ago. Our hearts will join Mary and Joseph in the stable, the shepherds on the hillside, and the Wise Men from the East as they come to Bethlehem. But to do this we must prepare. We must prepare as completely and as well as did the Palm Sunday worshipers. They knew He was coming and got ready. We also know He is coming. Let us get ready. Then we'll have a "prepared for" Palm Sunday — in Advent.

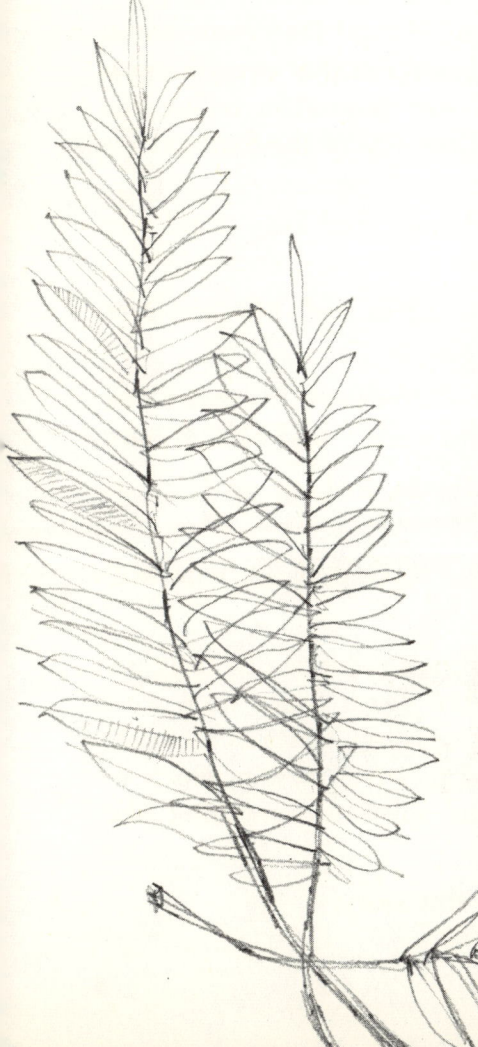

We usually come together to worship God by reading His Word and talking to Him in prayer. Tonight we want to worship God by working on something called a crèche (pronounced *kresh*).

The Crèche

FIRST WEEK IN ADVENT
Thursday

Preparation Project

A crèche is a reminder of the Holy Family as they might have appeared in Bethlehem on the night of Jesus' birth. The central figures are Mary, Joseph, and Jesus.

We like to join together as a family in making the crèche. We help each other put the pieces together because we love to thank God for His great Gift, Christ Jesus. After it is finished, the crèche will be a reminder to us.

The message of the crèche will be: "As did Mary, Joseph, the shepherds, and the Wise Men, worship your Lord."

Our time spent in making the crèche is worship when we give it to God because we love Him.

Prayer:

Dear God, bless our family as we make this model of the first Christmas. Remind us that You came into this world as a Child for us. Bless our crèche to help others in seeing Jesus as your Gift to us. Amen.

(Directions for making the crèche may be found on page 41.)

Do porpoises talk? A lot of people think they do. Scientists in Florida and California are recording the noises these fish make and are now trying to decipher them. But until these sounds are understood, they will only be more noise in an already noisy world.

Contrite

FIRST WEEK IN ADVENT
Friday
Isaiah 66:1, 2

A Preparation Word

When God wants to tell us something, He doesn't make noises which we in turn must try to decipher. He speaks to us clearly in words that can be understood. As we get ready for Christmas, we shall want to carefully study some words God has given us which will help us truly prepare. What better word to begin with, as our first preparation word, than "contrite"?

Contrite really means "bruised or crushed." If we were to take a big rock and smash it to powder, we could say we made it contrite. But contrite isn't a word which we normally use when speaking of stones. It's a word we use about people. God says He likes and wants contrite people. What could this mean?

When a child of God is truly saddened by the realization of his sin and truly sorry for what he has done against God, he is contrite. A contrite person admits his wrongs and is searching for forgiveness. God will make sure that we find it. Yet how will a person become contrite? Can he do it by himself?

No, God sends His Holy Spirit into our hearts. He leads us to contrition. He shows us our sin. But more than that, He shows us our Savior. If by the Holy Spirit's work we are contrite, God tells us, "To this man will I look, even to him that is poor and of a contrite spirit." He will look to us and say again, as He did from the cross, "Father, forgive them." And God in Christ will forgive. We prepare for Christmas joy by being contrite.

Prayer:

Lord, we fail You so often. How can we ever hope to prepare for a proper remembrance of Christ's birth? Send Your Holy Spirit to us that through Him we may be led from contrition to forgiveness to preparation. In Jesus' name. Amen.

The Psalms were the songbook of God's Old Testament people. New Testament Christians still find in them eternal truths about our changeless God. There are many different kinds of psalms. One kind we call antiphonal (an-TIF-un-ul) psalms. This means that one person or group of persons would speak part of the psalm while another person or group of persons would answer with the next part of the psalm. Psalm 24 was used as an antiphonal psalm. It was usually sung or said during the yearly journey to Jerusalem, where people went to worship in the temple. Through this psalm there breathes

"The King of Glory Comes"

FIRST WEEK
IN ADVENT
Saturday
Psalm 24

A Preparation Psalm

a spirit of intense anticipation. The travelers can hardly wait to get there. Thinking about the joy of worship and the wonder of the God they worshiped, the people would cry out, "Lift up your heads, O ye gates, and be ye lifted up, ye everlasting doors, and the King of Glory shall come in." What they are saying is, "Swing the doors wide open, as wide open as you can. Let the top of the doorway (the heads) be lifted up. Make a large entranceway. Let our great God in! To do this we will need the biggest opening possible!" Perhaps we can get the feel of this psalm if we say it antiphonally. *To do so, divide the family in two sections, and read it responsively.*

Group 1: (Verses 1 and 2)
    The earth is the Lord's and the fullness thereof, the world and they that dwell therein. For He hath founded it upon the seas and established it upon the floods.

Group 2: (Verse 3)
    (A voice) Who shall ascend into the hill of the Lord, or who shall stand in His holy place?

Group 1: (Verses 4, 5, 6)
    (Answering) He that hath clean hands and a pure heart, who hath not lifted up his soul unto vanity nor sworn deceitfully. He shall receive the blessing from the Lord, and righteousness from the God of his salvation. This is the generation of them that seek Him, that seek thy face, O Jacob.

Group 2: (Verse 7)
    (As they come closer to the temple) Lift up your heads, O ye gates; and be ye lifted up, ye everlasting doors; and the King of Glory shall come in.

Group 1: (Verse 8a)
    (A voice from the temple gates) Who is this King of Glory?

Group 2: (Verses 8b and 9)
> The Lord strong and mighty, the Lord mighty in battle. (Pause) Lift up your heads, O ye gates; even lift them up, ye everlasting doors; and the King of Glory shall come in.

Group 1: (Verse 10a)
> Who is this King of Glory?

Group 2: (Verse 10b)
> The Lord of hosts, He is the King of Glory.

This same psalm has been used by Christians as they approached Christmas. It is an Advent psalm. Why does it fit so well? Let's talk about it.

Prayer:

O Lord, as we reach the end of our first week of Christmas preparation, we give You thanks for our growing understanding. Help us to walk ever closer to You. May our Christmas this year be filled with the joy You offer all men in Christ Jesus. Through Your Holy Spirit help us grow during this Advent season. Lead us to open our hearts and home to Jesus, our Savior. Amen.

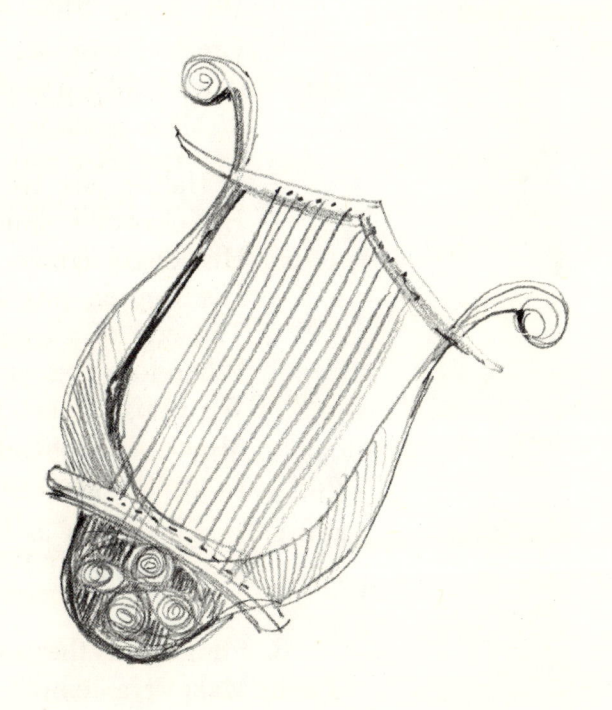

Yesterday our devotion centered on one of the great psalms of God's people, Psalm 24. Remember the verse, "Lift up your heads, O ye gates, and be ye lifted up, ye everlasting doors, and the King of Glory shall come in"? What went through your mind when you heard those words? When George Weissel heard these words more than 320 years ago, a hymn began to form in his mind. In time he

"Lift Up Your Heads, Ye Mighty Gates"

SECOND WEEK
IN ADVENT
Sunday
Psalm 24

A Preparation Hymn

wrote his thoughts about Psalm 24 down, and we now know them as one of the most thrilling of Advent's anticipation hymns, "Lift Up Your Heads, Ye Mighty Gates." Let us read through four of the stanzas and see if we can put into our own words what he stated in his.

1. Lift up your heads, ye mighty gates!
   Behold, the King of Glory waits;
   The King of kings is drawing near,
   The Savior of the world is here.
   Life and salvation He doth bring,
   Wherefore rejoice and gladly sing:
   We praise Thee, Father, now,
   Creator, wise art Thou!

Why do we praise the Father?

2. A Helper just He comes to thee,
   His chariot is humility,
   His kingly crown is holiness,
   His scepter, pity in distress.
   The end of all our woe He brings;
   Wherefore the earth is glad and sings:
   We praise Thee, Savior, now,
   Mighty in deed art Thou!

Kings of old rode in royal chariots, wore a brilliantly jeweled crown, and carried a scepter as a mark of power. According to this stanza, what special marks of kingship does the Savior have?

3. Fling wide the portals of your heart;
   Make it a temple set apart
   From earthly use for Heaven's employ,
   Adorned with prayer and love and joy.
   So shall your Sovereign enter in
   And new and nobler life begin.
   To Thee, O God, be praise
   For word and deed and grace!

The King needs a special place in which to live. What special place do we have for Him, and how may we properly prepare it?

4. Redeemer, come! I open wide
   My heart to Thee; here, Lord, abide!
   Let me Thine inner presence feel,
   Thy grace and love in me reveal;
   Thy Holy Spirit guide us on
   Until our glorious goal is won.
   Eternal praise and fame
   We offer to Thy name.

How can we feel God's grace, love, and inner presence? Now let us sing this hymn.

"What was God doing before creation?" little Amy asked.

"He was getting ready," answered Mrs. Wade.

"Getting ready? Getting ready for what?" said Amy with a puzzled frown.

"Getting ready for us, Amy. Getting ready for us," came Mrs. Wade's beautiful reply.

Noah and God's Ark

SECOND WEEK
IN ADVENT
Monday
Genesis 7:5-18

God Prepared for Man

Getting ready for us. That's right. And when the right moment came, He made the world and put everything in its place. And then when all that was finished, He said, "Let Us make man," and He did. That's how man came to live in a perfect world. God made it that way. There was nothing wrong with it then. Everything was just right.

How sad that sin came into the world to tear its perfection apart and stamp its beauty into the mud! Man, led by sin, did just that. Man wanted to go his own way. He wanted to walk with God no longer. Things finally got so bad that the Bible tells us, "Every imagination of the thoughts of his [man's] heart was only evil continually." God's perfect creation was ruined. It was marred beyond recall; all of it except Noah and his family. They alone in all the earth still trusted God and loved Him. But God knew that if He didn't do something quickly it was only a matter of time before there would be no one left who listened to His voice. So He acted. He decided to send a great flood and start life over. It wouldn't be the perfect world He had originally planned, but it would be a world in which His saving Word would lead many to life.

However, before this flood began, God once more prepared for man. He gave Noah instructions. He was to do two things. First of all, Noah was to preach righteousness, giving the people one more chance. If they repented, God would save them. Second, Noah was to build a special boat, planned by God, in which all kinds of living creatures were to be gathered. That way, after the flood, life could go on.

Right up to the last moment God was intent on saving His people. He wanted them all to turn to Him. That's why He told Noah to preach. If they wouldn't turn to Him, God was at least going to save Noah and his family. So we see that God continued His preparation for man, even after the first creation was finished. He was still looking out for His children.

Did God's concern stop after the flood? Not at all. The nearness of Jesus' birthday reminds us that His love continued. Through the years He continued preparing for man. The reason we are preparing for Christmas is because God first prepared Christmas for us.

"Sherri, Sherri! Whatever is wrong? Why are you crying? It's almost Christmastime. The children's service is about to begin. This is no time for tears!"

A Gift for Jesus

SECOND WEEK IN ADVENT
Tuesday

A Preparation Open-End Story

Mrs. Abel, Sherri Pierce's Sunday school teacher, was talking to one of her pupils. Down in the basement of the church all was excitement. Children were talking and laughing; teachers were trying to get classes lined up; the superintendent was issuing last-minute instructions, and parents, out of breath, were bringing their children through the door just in the nick of time. Everyone was happy and chattering. Everyone but Sherri.

"Oh, Mrs. Abel! I don't have anything to put in the manger for Jesus," said Sherri between sobs.

That sounds strange to us, but Mrs. Abel knew what she meant. The Sunday school children had been asked to bring a special offering for Christ's work on the night of their Christmas service. After each class had recited or sung, they were going to put their offering in the manger as a Christmas present for the One who was God's Present to us.

"Did you lose it? Don't worry. I'm sure it will be found. Even if it isn't, I'll give you something to put in the manger," said Mrs. Abel reassuringly.

"No! No, Mrs. Abel," Sherri interrupted, "I didn't lose it. I — I gave it away. I wanted to bring a gift that I had earned myself. I didn't want money my mother and father had given me. So I earned this dollar, and then I just gave my present away."

"Gave it away?" said Mrs. Abel. "What do you mean?"

"Well, I had a dollar saved. It was five dimes and two quarters. I had it all saved a week ago. Then last week I was in a store. On the counter was one of those little cans they use for collecting money. It had a sign on it that said this can was for helping people who have multiple sclerosis. Jean, my next-door neighbor, told me they just found out her favorite uncle had that. So I decided that I would put one of the quarters in that can. Jean's my best friend, and I thought it would make her feel good and might even help. Then last week at school the teacher told of some children she knew whose father was sick. They didn't have any warm clothes and wouldn't have any Christmas this year. So I gave the other quarter to her for them. I kept thinking all the time that I would find some way to earn the money again, but I just couldn't find a way. Day before yesterday Georgie, my brother, told me that he had found a wonderful present for Mom. Only he needed fifty cents more to get it. Well,

17

I started thinking how much Mom would like what he wanted to buy, and I gave him the fifty cents. Now I don't have anything left. I gave Jesus' gift away. I have nothing to bring Him."

"Oh, Sherri," said Mrs. Abel, "don't cry about what you did. You didn't give Jesus' gift away."

Now let's prepare a proper ending.

(After some discussion the leader might want to read aloud Matthew 25:34-40)

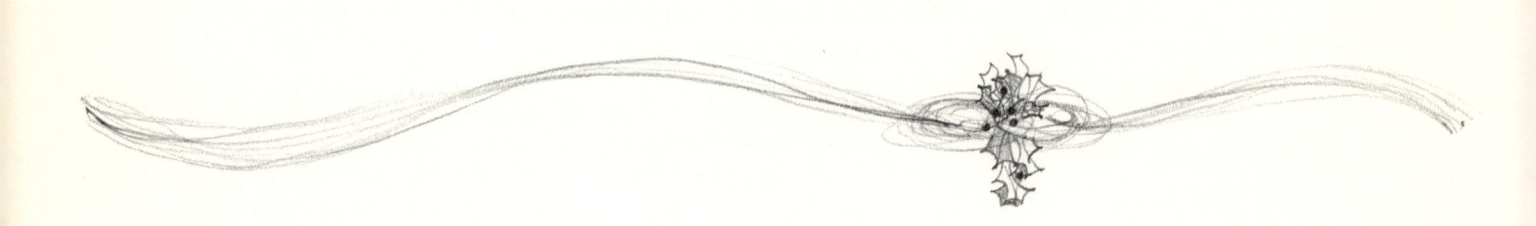

When Preparation Is an Insult

SECOND WEEK
IN ADVENT
Wednesday
Exodus 40:1-16

Men Who Prepared for God

It may sound strange, but there are times when preparation is an insult. That's right — an insult. A man once insulted Jesus in this way. Jesus visited this man's house by invitation (Luke 7:44-47), but the man didn't really prepare for Him. The man brought Jesus in but did almost nothing to show Jesus that He was welcome. He said the right words — with no feeling of sincerity. The man insulted Christ by his scanty preparation and minimum courtesy, even though there was time and opportunity to do better. This is no way to treat a friend, especially when that friend is God.

God's people of the Old Testament knew and understood this. They knew that preparation for God demanded their best and that getting ready for a proper worship of God was hard work. In Exodus 40 God makes this clear by saying, "When you come to worship Me, make certain that everything is in order. No matter how much work it takes, put everything needed for honoring Me in the right place. When all things are ready, the priests may clean themselves and put on their special clothes to come into My house. Then, properly prepared, give Me praise."

When we read the chapters of Exodus that go before this, we see how carefully everything needed for worshiping God is described. Gold, silver, rich materials, costly jewels were all used in making the special equipment. No one could get away with casually slouching

18

into the presence of the Lord. God wouldn't stand for it. The people who loved Him wouldn't permit it. In the Old Testament God's people spared no effort when making preparation for Him.

But what about today? What is the quality of preparation for service to God among God's children today? How carefully are Christian Christmas preparations being made? How carefully are they being made by us? These are questions we must ask — and answer.

We are coming to Christmas. God prepared the first Christmas for us. No insult could be read into His preparation. He gave the very best, His only Son. Now we prepare for a proper remembering of this first Christmas. Could God be insulted by our preparation? Should He be? Let's talk about it. Let's wrestle with the question: Did the Old Testament children of God, who had only a promise of a Savior, prepare better for their Lord than we New Testament Christians who know that Jesus Christ came?

Prayer:

Come, Lord. Prepare our hearts to properly prepare for You. Amen.

The Crèche

SECOND WEEK IN ADVENT
Thursday

Preparation Project

Our crèche helps us remember the coming of Jesus to earth as our Savior and Brother.

But we want to do more than remember the birth of Jesus. We can use the crèche to help us share the good news of Christmas during these days. By itself the crèche will say that we think the coming of Christ is very important. If we go one step farther, we can also say why we think His coming is so great.

We can explain the meaning of Jesus and His birth in our life. The angel said to the shepherds, "I bring you good tidings of great joy which shall be to all people."

Shall we talk about how we can share Christ Jesus and the news of His birth this Christmas?

Prayer:

O Lord, as our fingers work to make this crèche, help us to feel the joy of everything You have made for us. Teach our tongues to tell the Good News of Christ Jesus to others. Be with us and all Christians to bring the story of Jesus to the whole world. Amen.

What's the hardest thing in the world to do? Climb a mountain? Get an *A* in English? Make a million dollars? All those things are difficult but not the hardest thing to do. The hardest thing in the world to do is to repent. Why? Because no man can do it — not by himself. It takes God's full power working in a man to make repenting possible. Let's talk about why repenting is so difficult and still so very important.

Repent

SECOND WEEK IN ADVENT
Friday
Acts 2:37-39

A Preparation Word

John the Baptist, Christ's way-preparer, really had only a one-sentence message to preach: "Repent ye, for the kingdom of heaven is at hand" (Matthew 3:2). Jesus later called for the same thing: "Except ye repent, ye shall all . . . perish" (Luke 13:3). This message, whether preached by John or by Jesus, made people angry. They became angry because "repent" means to have a change of mind or heart. Before a person repents, he must admit that his old way has been a wrong way. Only then can he change, for only then will he have reason to change.

But how do we lead a man to repentance? We may argue with him all we want; we may point out his mistake so clearly that even a fool could see it; we can show him exactly what is wrong, but these things won't make him repent. Only One can make a man repent. That One is God the Holy Spirit. The Spirit must come into a man's heart and turn it to faith. Jeremiah put his finger on it when he prayed, "Turn Thou me and I shall be turned" (Jeremiah 31:18). God alone can do this. It is about the most important thing that can happen to us. Jesus said, "Except ye be converted [turned] . . . ye shall not enter into the kingdom of heaven." (Matthew 18:3)

As we near Christmas, we can see all the more clearly the need for this change of mind in all of us. Listen as people talk. Hear what they are saying. Their speech is full of wants for themselves, and their language is peppered with "I's" and "me's" and "mine's." This is a time when we should overflow with "You's" and "Christ's" and "His"! It will certainly take a change of mind this Christmas to put the emphasis where it belongs. It *is* Christ's birthday. We *are* celebrating the birth of God's Son, who came to take away man's sin. It is time for us to say again, "Father, I have sinned against heaven and in Your sight. I am no more worthy to be called Your son." That's not a bad sentence. It's a truly wonderful one, for it can be spoken only by a repentant Christian. After we have said it, God always answers, "Be of good cheer, My child, your sins are forgiven you."

Some people don't like the psalms. They feel that the language is unclear and the words don't make sense. One of the reasons they feel this way is that they read the psalms as if they were a page from a dull schoolbook. Actually the psalms are more like a picture album. They must be read that way. Psalm 91 is an example of this. Let's talk about that psalm today.

A Christian Picture Book

SECOND WEEK IN ADVENT
Saturday
Psalm 91

A Preparation Psalm

As we look at Psalm 91, remember our devotion of yesterday on the word "repent." This psalm was written by a man who had repented, whose outlook on life was changed. He was a man who knew what repentance meant. God had turned this man to the way of trust. In the first 13 verses the writer draws 18 pictures of how God takes care of His own. Eighteen times he says, "I'm a changed man, O Lord, I trust You." The first two pictures are in verse one. In that verse the holy writer says, "God is like a great cave into which I can go for safety and protection. God is also like a big rock that casts its cool shadow for me to rest in at high noon." Let's see how many of the 18 pictures of trust we can find painted in the next 12 verses. *(Talk about it)*

In verses 14—16 God is speaking. He speaks words of wonderful promise. In these verses God makes eight promises to His trusting child. He says, "I will deliver him"; "I will protect him"; "I will answer him"; "I will be with him"; "I will rescue him"; "I will honor him"; "I will satisfy him"; "I will show him My salvation." God does this for all of His repentant, trusting children. He fulfills these eight promises by giving us a Savior. This Savior, Jesus Christ, does all of these things. He is our reason for Christmas.

Let us pray God to keep us changed through repentance that we may trust in Him and His Christmas act of love.

Prayer:

As we close our second week of Christmas preparation, cause our sense of awe and expectancy to grow. Let Christ live in our heart and home. Lead us down the road of repentance to a trusting faith and sure happiness in You. Amen.

Twelve hundred years ago a beautiful Advent hymn was written. No one knows who wrote the words and the music to this marvelous hymn of Christmas preparation. But isn't it exciting to know that Christians have used this music and these words for such a very long time? This ancient hymn we now call "Oh, Come, Oh, Come, Emmanuel."

"Oh, Come, Oh, Come, Emmanuel"

THIRD WEEK IN ADVENT
Sunday

A Preparation Hymn

This hymn, like Psalm 24 (Saturday, first week in Advent), was used antiphonally. One group sang the first two lines, another sang the third and fourth, and then all joined to sing, "Rejoice! Rejoice! Emmanuel Shall come to thee, O Israel." At the close of our devotion let us divide into two groups and sing the hymn antiphonally.

But let us first see what these stanzas are saying to us.

1. Oh, come, oh, come, Emmanuel,
   And ranson captive Israel
   That mourns in lonely exile here
   Until the Son of God appear.
   Rejoice! Rejoice! Emmanuel
   Shall come to thee, O Israel.

Stanza 1 is a plea for release. The writer remembers how God's Old Testament people were held captive for 70 years in Babylon. How they must have yearned to be delivered and to return to their homeland! This stanza reminds us that we are sin's captives until — until who comes?

2. Oh, come, Thou Rod of Jesse, free
   Thine own from Satan's tyranny;
   From depths of hell Thy people save
   And give them victory o'er the grave.
   Rejoice! Rejoice! Emmanuel
   Shall come to thee, O Israel.

The second stanza sparkles with an Easter flavor. It says the same thing as 1 Corinthians 15:54-57, where we are told that Christ by His resurrection took the sting out of death; it has no lasting power over us. The "Rod of Jesse" is Jesus. Rod means a little shoot or a sprig. Jesse, the father of King David, was the family group from which the Messiah was to come. "There shall come forth a rod out of the stem of Jesse, and a Branch shall grow out of his roots" (Isaiah 11:1). Could we agree that Christmas is the doorway to Easter?

3. Oh, come, Thou Dayspring from on high,
   And cheer us by Thy drawing nigh;

Disperse the gloomy clouds of night
And death's dark shadows put to flight.
Rejoice! Rejoice! Emmanuel
Shall come to thee, O Israel.

A "dayspring" is a dawning. As each new day springs into being by chasing away the dark of night and bringing light, so the new day of the Sun of Righteousness brings shining brightness and hope to all the people who sat in the night of sin. Simeon called Jesus the Dayspring (Luke 1:78) when he said: ". . . whereby the Dayspring from on high hath visited us, to give light to them that sit in darkness." How does Jesus brighten our lives?

4. Oh, come, Thou Key of David, come
And open wide our heavenly home;
Make safe the way that leads on high,
And close the path to misery.
Rejoice! Rejoice! Emmanuel
Shall come to thee, O Israel.

In this last stanza Jesus is called the Key of David. A key is used to open a locked door. Christ, by His act of redeeming us, opened heaven's door to all men. We can enter our Father's house because He made it possible.

In this hymn are four pictures of Christ's accomplishments for us. Because He did these things, we call Him Emmanuel, which means "God-with-us." At Christmas Christians pray: "This Christmas come to us, God-with-us."

Now let us sing this thrilling preparation hymn.

As Christians we never forget how carefully God prepared for man. We remember the marvel of creation and how perfectly everything was put together. This was all done for us. But Satan almost destroyed that perfect world when he brought in sin. Even after sin had marred the original beauty, God let man live on in a still thrilling but imperfect universe. However, Satan continued to work his cruel and clever plan for drawing the creature, man, away from the Creator, God. Once more Satan almost succeeded. Another generation or

God's Kingdom Prepared for You

THIRD WEEK
IN ADVENT
Monday
Matthew 25:31-34

God Prepared for Man

two after Noah and it may well have been that there would have been no man living to honor and worship the Lord. So the Lord sent the flood and began again, though not before first preparing an escape for His faithful few, Noah and his family.

We could trace God's hand of deliverance through the history of the world. We could show how time and again, like the hero in a melodrama, God comes through at the moment of man's greatest need with just the answer required to save the hour. God was and is always prepared to answer our cry for help. Even before we call, He is preparing the answer. While we are wrestling with just how to say what is on our mind, God's perfect response is already falling in place.

But why? Why does God care? Our answer from Scripture is a thing of beauty. We are told, "God is Love." We are told He loves us. He loves us not because of what we are but because of who He is. He is Love.

His love for us makes Him prepare for our every need. The greatest need we have is the need for a place with Him. We need a place with Him both now and through all eternity. That, too, has long been prepared for us. Jesus, speaking to those who appear before His throne of judgment, says: "Come, ye blessed of My Father, inherit the Kingdom prepared for you from the foundation of the world." God prepared that kingdom from the first moments of time. God prepared it for us.

Because God prepared for us, we have much reason to prepare for Him this Christmas. We remember what He did. We are reminded of His careful and complete concern for our every need. He prepared for us. He prepared everything needed for us. From the very beginning He prepared a place for us in His kingdom. Through His Son we are now part of His kingdom. We have reason to prepare for every Christmas because God first prepared for us from the foundation of the world.

"That's what Dad said. I heard him. No use complaining about it. You know Dad. Once he makes up his mind, nothing can change it — except maybe Mom — sometimes."

No Presents This Christmas

THIRD WEEK IN ADVENT
Tuesday

A Preparation Story

Doug was talking to Mike and Tom about what he considered the worst thing that had ever happened to their family. His father had told his mother, while he was eavesdropping, that this year there would be no Christmas gifts for the family. It wasn't that they couldn't afford gifts. He said that the Christmas presents had gotten out of hand. Each year there seemed to be more and more presents and less and less Christ in their Christmas celebration. That's what Doug's dad said. You can imagine how blue the boys were when they heard about that!

Next morning, around the breakfast table, the gloom was so thick not even an army tank could blast its way through. Tom moped. Mike pouted. Doug trembled on the edge of tears. It didn't take Mr. Humes two minutes to feel the mood of his boys.

"Good morning! Everybody slept well? My, it's nice to see so many cheery faces. Does a man's heart good to come down to breakfast and see everyone just bubbling over with happiness. By the way, who died?" he asked his wife.

"I think someone overheard what we talked about last night," she answered.

"Oh! So that's it. Well, we might as well talk about it now. If one of you heard that we decided there would be no Christmas presents this year, you heard right. I'd like to explain to you why, though, if you'll all listen. Then, if you have anything to say, we'll talk about it."

Mr. Humes tried to explain the reason for his decision. He spoke with them of what Jesus' birthday should mean. He spoke with them about the way the true reason for Christmas was slowly being pushed into the background. "Now," he said, "most people didn't have even a glimmer of the real reason for the day." When he was done, the boys were silent.

"Anything you'd like to say, boys?" he asked.

"Yeah, Dad," said Tom. "I know all you say is true, but I still don't think it's fair to make us give up our Christmas presents. We go to church and Sunday school. We keep Christ in our Christmas. Why should we be deprived of presents and all the fun? What if we each get just two presents apiece? Wouldn't that be a kind of — uh, what do you call it — uh, a compromise?"

"I suppose so," said his dad, "but I still don't think you understand what I'm saying. There shouldn't be *any* gifts for us on this day. Whether it's two gifts or ten gifts is beside the point. That's not what Christmas is for. But I'll tell you what we'll do. Tonight when I get home we'll go see Pastor Kruger. Let's see what he has to say about it."

That evening in the pastor's study Mr. Humes explained what he wanted to do. The boys watched Pastor Kruger carefully for his reaction.

"Well, now," said Pastor Kruger, "that's a very interesting approach to Christmas. I think I would have to say that I both agree and disagree."

Now let's prepare a proper ending.

Unaware

THIRD WEEK
IN ADVENT
Wednesday
Exodus 3:1-11

Men Who Prepared for God

The Bible is filled with stories of men who prepared, willingly and sometimes unwillingly, for service to God. There were men like Abraham, Isaac, Jacob, and Joseph. Men like Isaiah, Jeremiah, Ezekiel, and Daniel, like Peter, James, John, and Paul. These are but a few of the men who prepared for service to God. But there is one man in the Bible who spent almost a lifetime preparing to serve God without really being aware of what he was doing. This man is Moses.

Most Christians know about Moses and the strange life he led. At birth he was hidden in a little basket and set afloat on the Nile, only to be discovered by Pharaoh's daughter. He was raised in Pharaoh's palace and received an excellent education. The Book of Acts says: "And Moses was instructed in all the wisdom of the Egyptians." But Moses sinned against man and God when he committed murder. He had to flee to the land of Midian. At that time he was in the prime of life, 40 years old. He stayed in Midian 40 more years, making his living as a herdsman.

If someone had asked Moses at the end of his 40 years of herding cattle (he was then 80 years old) what he was preparing to be in life, Moses might have said, "Preparing to be? Ridiculous! I'm not preparing to be anything. My life is about over. All that is left for me is to die and return to God. Oh, no, I'm not preparing anymore. My preparation days are far behind me."

26

But it wasn't so. Moses hadn't even begun to do all that God had in store for him. His first 80 years were but the opening chapter in a very long and very full book of life. He was preparing for a special service and didn't know it. Before him yet, at 80 years of age, was his great work of leading the Children of Israel out of Egypt to the borders of the Promised Land.

Preparing isn't always something we consciously do. We aren't always aware of those things for which our activities make us ready. Many a child attending Christian classes is actually getting ready for a lifetime in the teaching and preaching ministry of the church. Years ago most of us learned hymns and Scripture readings which prepared us to make this Christmas a Christ-centered celebration. People who make Christian Christmas decorations often discover that they are setting the stage for telling someone else of the wonder of the Savior. We prepare — unaware. We prepare unaware because God gives us opportunities for witness, worship, and service which we, in our wildest dreams, hardly imagine.

(This would be a good time to invite members of the family to relate instances in their life where they had prepared unaware for special service.)

Let us ask for God's Holy Spirit that we may be empowered to prepare, even though unaware, for His work. He tells us: "All things work together for good to them that love God." (Romans 8:28) That also includes all Christian preparation, even when it becomes a part of our life, unaware.

Prayer:

Lord, prepare me to serve You. Use me for glorifying my Savior among men. Amen.

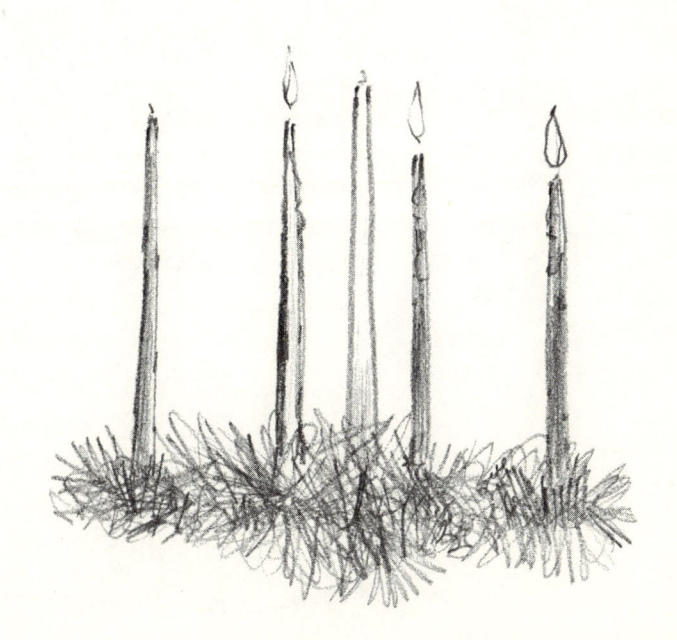

The Christmas tree is the center of nearly every house in these wonderful days. We like to think of its meaning.

The green Christmas tree shows the everlasting love of God. Alive all year, it also shows the Christian's life active in God's service.

The Christmas Tree Base

THIRD WEEK IN ADVENT
Thursday

Preparation Project

love every day. The bright ornaments remind us of the gifts which the Wise Men brought to Jesus. The lights tell us that Christ is the Light of the world.

We can help make the Christmas tree more beautiful by making a tree base. This is something we can make together as a family.

Making the Christmas tree base is a way of worshiping God. We do our work together to love God and praise Him for the birth of Jesus.

Prayer:

We ask you to bless our family, O Lord, as we come together to make something for our Christmas celebration. Amen.

(Directions for making the Christmas tree base may be found on page 47.)

Many of the words which we use in everyday speech have differing meanings. Think of the word "catch," for instance. We catch a train, catch a cold, catch a ball, and often ask, "Do you catch on?" See the differing meanings? Our preparation word for today, "grace," is another word with many uses. It may be a girl's name; it may describe a person who moves with ease and beauty; we even sometimes address certain noblemen as "Your Grace."

To a Christian, grace has a quite different meaning. It describes to us God's reason for loving us. Grace is God's favor to man, undeserved by us. He loves us not because of what we are but because

Grace

THIRD WEEK
IN ADVENT
Friday
John 1:14-17

A Preparation Word

of what He is. This loving concern for us which overlooks our many apparent faults and keeps on loving we call grace. Because God looks to us through eyes of grace He does not destroy us when we sin but speaks to us of forgiveness. God's grace makes forgiveness possible.

John tells us in the first chapter of his gospel that when the Word (Jesus) came, He was full of grace. His life was a life of active grace, for He said that He was not come to the "righteous" in life, but He came to call sinners to repentance. He knew they were sinners when He came. Because He was full of grace, He saw past their sinfulness to their need. Only a God of grace could do that.

We can't understand this wonderful part of God. That isn't possible! Only God knows *why* He is full of grace toward us. We can only rejoice that it is true and trust His grace.

This Christmas we will sing with the angels, "Unto you is born this day in the city of David a Savior, which is Christ the Lord." He's come. That's what is important. He came because God is a God of grace. He came bringing God's never-ending and never-changing grace to all mankind. He proved God's grace for us, for if He did not love us dearly, would He send His Son to bear our sins?

Christmas is nearer. It comes to us in Christ. We come to it in faith. The road by which a true Christmas comes to us and we go to meet it is the same road. It has a name. The name is Grace. If we walk the Grace Road, we shall find God's Christmas come to us and we shall rejoice that the Bearer of God's Grace is born. We shall behold His glory, full of grace.

Prayer:

We know we are saved by grace, Lord. Let us never forget the thrilling beauty of this word. May we never fail to lean upon its meaning and depend on its promise. In Jesus' name. Amen.

Many people have a strange picture of God. If we were to actually draw a cartoon of it, we should sketch a little, old man hunched over a huge ledger book. In his hand is poised a pen, and over his eyes is the kind of green visor that old-time bookkeepers wore. From time to time he peers around the edge of the book down toward earth,

Does God Keep Score?

THIRD WEEK IN ADVENT
Saturday
Psalm 130

A Preparation Psalm

where all mankind is busy living out their lives. After each peek he rustles through the pages to a particular name and makes a check behind it. Night and day, week in and week out the little, old bookkeeper stays at it, marking down all the good and all the bad done by all men. If this were actually a true picture of God, we should all be in trouble. But this isn't God. This is more of a picture of Santa Claus. Remember the lines from "Santa Claus Is Coming to Town"?

>He's making a list and checking it twice,
>He's gonna find out who's naughty or nice.
>Santa Claus is coming to town.

That's how Santa may act, but not God.

David asks a very important question in Psalm 130. He asks: "If Thou, Lord, shouldest mark iniquities, O Lord, who shall stand?" What he is saying is this: If God were a scorekeeper, who wouldn't be in trouble? All have sinned. All have failed. All would be rejected if God were a scorekeeper. But He isn't.

God is a God of grace. He gives us pardon — gives it even though we have done nothing to deserve it.

"I wait for the Lord, my soul doth wait." When David thought of his wonderful God, who isn't a mere scorekeeper, he yearned to meet Him. Why? Because when the Lord comes, He comes with mercy, forgiveness, healing, and hope. He brings these things because He is full of grace.

Let us rejoice that we shall once more have a chance to celebrate the coming of the King with healing in His wings of mercy and grace.

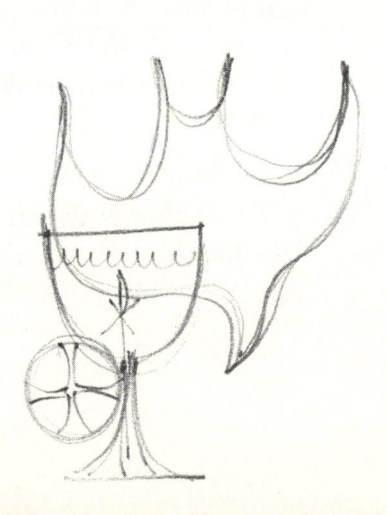

In our nation's capital, Washington, D. C., traffic is often interrupted by a motorcycle policeman with lights flashing and siren screaming. Following him are one or two other policemen and finally a large limousine. In the automobile may be the President of the United States or some other important official of the Government. The policemen who speed their motorcycles before the limousine are important. They prepare the way and announce that someone of greater importance is coming.

"On Jordan's Bank the Baptist's Cry"

FOURTH WEEK IN ADVENT
Sunday
Matthew 3:1-3

A Preparation Hymn

When God sent His Son into the world, He sent a sort of motorcycle escort before the Savior. The escort wasn't a group of uniformed policemen; it was one man. He didn't come with screaming siren and flashing lights. He came rather quietly. But like the modern motorcycle escort, he had a very important task. He was to say, "The Lord is near!"

Our preparation hymn for this last Sunday has the flavor of the motorcycle escort. It reminds us of the mission of John the Baptist, the preparer. Let us talk about this wonderful hymn.

1. On Jordan's bank the Baptist's cry
   Announces that the Lord is nigh;
   Come, then, and hearken, for he brings
   Glad tidings from the King of kings.

This stanza tells what John the Baptist did and what we in turn are to do. How could we state this stanza's meaning?

2. Then cleansed be every Christian breast
   And furnished for so great a Guest.
   Yea, let us each our hearts prepare
   For Christ to come and enter there.

Before Christ comes we must do some housecleaning. What ought to be cleaned?

3. For Thou art our Salvation, Lord,
   Our Refuge, and our great Reward.
   Without Thy grace our souls must fade
   And wither like a flower decayed.

How important Christ is! Just how important does the stanza say Christ is?

4. All praise, eternal Son, to Thee,
   Whose advent sets Thy people free,
   Whom, with the Father, we adore
   And Holy Ghost forevermore.

Christ's coming sets people free. How?

Now let us sing this hymn of praise and preparation.

(The Advent season varies in length, depending on the day Christmas falls. The devotions are prepared for the maximum length of Advent. When Christmas falls on any day but Sunday, follow the devotions in the book to Dec. 23, then turn to the Christmas Eve and Christmas Day devotions for use on Dec. 24 and 25.)

Preparing the Preparer

FOURTH WEEK IN ADVENT
Monday
Luke 1:5-23 and 57-64

God Prepared for Man

Most people call Jesus' cousin "John the Baptist." That's not a bad name, but is it the best? Maybe he ought to be called something else, something like "John the Preparer," for that was His most important purpose in life. God sent him to prepare the people for Jesus' coming. John told them: "Get ready, the Lamb of God who will take away the sins of the world is coming." Reading about him in the Bible, we see that he faithfully fulfilled this purpose in life. He preached repentance and preparation, getting the people ready for the appearance of Christ. John the Baptist can most certainly also be called John the Preparer.

When we think about John, it is easy to forget something that is very important. We tend to forget that *God* was the One who actually made the preparation. He prepared the preparer. It was God who first of all determined that it was time for the preparer. He sent an angel to John's parents, Zacharias and Elizabeth, telling them that they would have a son. He told them what to name him and outlined his purpose for life. God then gave them the promised son. John grew up strong and sturdy in body and spirit until the day that his mission in life was to begin. That day came. In Luke 3:2 we are told that God spoke to John while he was living in the wilderness. What did God tell him? God told him it was time to begin his great work. John obeyed God and in so doing fulfilled a prophecy given by Isaiah many years before: "The voice of him that crieth in the wilderness, Prepare ye the way of the Lord" (Isaiah 40:3). John fulfilled his purpose in life. He prepared for Christ. But it was God who first prepared John. Behind all of John's preparation was God — preparing.

We are now on the very edge of Christmas. Even here God is speaking to us, saying: "If you haven't prepared before, prepare now. There is still time. Be contrite, repent, and seek My grace. In My Savior Son I will give you all that you need, more than you can use. I give you peace, hope, happiness, and joy through the forgiveness He has earned for you. Prepare for Him. I prepared for you. If you will let Me, I will prepare you as I did John the Baptist." John the Preparer prepared people for the coming of Christ. But God prepared John the Preparer.

Prayer:

Dear Lord, as we stand here face to face with Christmas, lead us to give our hearts to You. In Christ Jesus wipe away our sins of selfishness, pride, and ingratitude. Make this Christmas a true spiritual experience that we may rejoice in You and Your Gift. Amen.

It was the week before Christmas, and Pastor Birner was tired — dead tired. He had been working hard and long to prepare himself and his congregation for a Christian Christmas. Even before Advent began, he had been drafting letters, setting up special services, writing sermons, and printing the bulletins for use by the congregation in the pre-Christmas and Christmas season. Time and again, in what he said and what he wrote, he struck the same theme. Over and over again he told the people, "Christmas is Christ's birthday. Keep it that way!"

"I Give Up"

FOURTH WEEK IN ADVENT
Tuesday

Open-End Story

Whenever he said this, the congregation sympathetically nodded its agreement, assumed a position of pious horror at the terrible things the world was doing during the Christmas season, and then went right on encouraging these abuses by their wholehearted participation. People in his parish had the largest Christmas tree on their block, the gaudiest lawn decorations of Rudolf and his reindeer friends, the biggest packages with the brightest bows hidden away in their closets, awaiting Christmas morn.

Pastor Birner was deeply disturbed by all this, but not simply because he was tired. Oh, no! He was disturbed because he had worked so hard to overcome this trend away from a Christian Christmas, and he felt he was losing the battle. So at the church council meeting just a few days before Christmas he gave voice and vent to his inner frustration. When he expressed his feelings, his words were simple and direct: "I give up."

You could have heard a pin drop when he said that. Mr. Johnson looked at Mr. Watkins. Mr. Watkins nervously glanced at Mr. Schmidt. Mr. Schmidt just sat still. It was finally Mr. Miller, the chairman of the trustees, who spoke up.

"Pastor," he said, "we can understand your feelings, but you can't give up. We need you to keep struggling and battling on."

"Not I," answered Pastor Birner. "I quit. From now on I'm going to take care of my family and say all the right things for the congregation, but I'm not going to try to reverse the tide of Christmas abuse. The devil has Christmas. He can keep it."

Once again silence settled over the assembled men.

"You all look shocked at what I am saying. Don't be. I have done everything humanly possible to arouse a sense of Christian responsibility in the people of the congregation in this community. It has done no good. Today I received five Christmas cards in the mail. They were the straw that broke the camel's back. They were sent by members and might well have been sent by an atheist. Two had snow scenes and hoped that I would have a joyful holiday season and a prosperous New Year; one had a snowman with pipe in mouth that simply announced, 'Happy Holidays'; and the last two were a picture of that fat little fellow, all dressed in red, who cheerily told me that once more the season for family joys was upon us. Those weren't the first cards like that I have received, and I'm sure they won't be the last. After all the letters, announcements, and mention in the sermon to see that happen! When I got those cards, I gave up!"

When the pastor stopped talking, each man in the council quietly sat rummaging through his thoughts. Once again it was Mr. Miller who broke the stillness.

"I can see you feel very strongly about this, Pastor. I must confess that I never really understood before just how intense your feelings were. The silence that surrounds us tonight is probably a silence of guilt — at least it is with me. Just sitting here thinking about the whole problem has opened my eyes to things I had previously ignored or missed. But, Pastor, I still think you cannot quit. Not now. To succeed — and we must succeed — you will have to —"

Now let's prepare a proper ending.

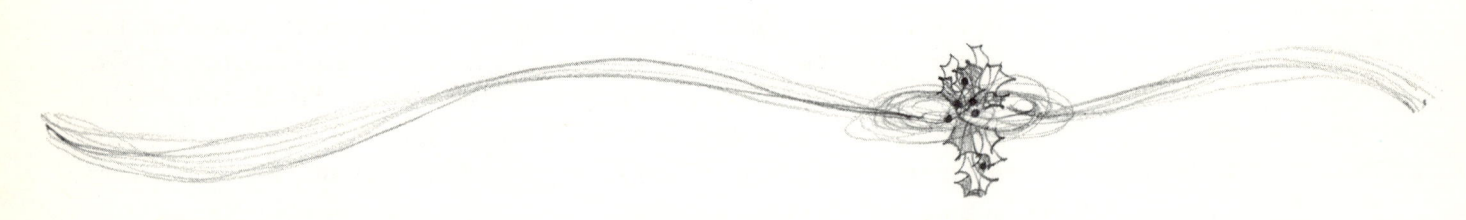

John the Baptist

FOURTH WEEK IN ADVENT
Wednesday
Luke 1:80; 3:1-3

Men Prepare to Serve God

This, the last week before Christmas, has certainly been John-the-Baptist week. Sunday's hymn spoke of John's work. Monday's devotion told of how God prepared John, who in turn prepared the people. Today we will take a closer look at John himself. In doing so we need to realize that while God prepared for us by sending this great man, this great man also prepared for his service to God.

John was Jesus' second cousin. He was born before Jesus. During most of his early years he lived in the wilderness. There in the quiet and solitude of the simple life he grew. He grew not only physically, but he also grew spiritually. There were other good men living in the wilderness. We can assume that they helped John in his faith life. God works in us through other men too. John did much personal study also. He searched the Scriptures and became familiar with all of God's revealed truth. He disciplined himself and lived a pure life. In every way he busied himself during the first 30 years of his life, preparing for the work God sent him into the world to do. John prepared for his service to God.

John wasn't the first man who prepared to serve God, nor was he the last. All who are truly God's children prepare for service to God. They bring Him the best they have in the best way they know. Nothing slipshod for God's people when they come to serve their Lord!

But what of us? What of us this Christmas? Are we prepared to receive the glad tidings of the Savior born with hearts bursting for joy? It will depend. It will depend on how we have prepared for His coming and for service to Him now and always. John prepared by prayer, meditation, communion with God, and discipline. Have we done the same? Let's talk about it.

Prayer:

Precious Savior, help us to continue our preparation for You and Your coming. May we be ready. Amen.

The Christmas Tree Base

FOURTH WEEK IN ADVENT
Thursday

Preparation Project

Worship is more than using words. Worship happens when God comes to us in His loving way through Jesus and makes us want to love Him with our heart, hands, and body.

We can use some things to help us show our love in worship. A cross, an Advent wreath, a crèche, a family altar, the Bible, prayerbooks, and pictures all help us to worship.

Our Christmas tree base is that kind of help. It helps us to be ready for sharing Christ with one another.

Shall we talk about it? How does it help us talk about God? How can we use it for sharing the love of Christ?

Prayer:

Open our lips, dear Father, to show Your praise. Help us to speak and live your love with one another in our family. Bless our gift giving and receiving, our family games and meals in the joy of Jesus' birth. Amen.

An advertising agency once made a study of which words in the English language persuaded people to buy. The list they finally gathered included the following familiar words: you, discover, easy, proven, save, money, guarantee, health, happiness, love, and results. It might be fun to see if we couldn't make a Christian sentence with those eleven words. One of the things we notice about this list is that so many of them are part and parcel of the Christian message. Some are used more often than others; some are more important to us than others. But of the entire list, one word stands out as the most important of all. That word is "save."

Save

FOURTH WEEK IN ADVENT
Friday
Matthew 1:18-21

A Preparation Word

When a farmer lost in the blizzard finds a house or barn, he is saved. When a young boy suddenly seized with a cramp while swimming is towed ashore by a lifeguard, he is saved. When a little girl who falls in the middle of a busy street is snatched from under the wheels of a moving truck, she is saved. All of those are important uses of the word "save." But the most important is this: When God sent His Son into the world to bear the sins of all men and then gives His Holy Spirit to them in order that they might believe, they are saved.

Save means rescue. Save means life and hope. Save means that help and a helper are here. All these meanings make "save" a Christmas word. Jesus came into the world and became man to "seek and to save that which was lost" (Luke 19:10). The angel told Joseph that Jesus would "save His people from their sins." He came to seek and to save. Save is an important word.

Two days to Christmas! Why do we rejoice? Why are our hearts glad? What makes us merry? Jesus came to save. Jesus came to save us.

> Hail, the heavenly Prince of Peace!
> Hail, the Sun of Righteousness!
> Light and life to all He brings,
> Risen with healing in His wings.
> Mild He leaves His throne on high,
> Born that man no more may die!
> Born to raise the sons of earth;
> Born to give them second birth.
> Hark! the herald angels sing,
> "Glory to the newborn King!"

(NOTE: For this devotion let the family gather around the Christmas tree. Divide this order of service so that each one participates in some way. The very little child may begin the service by saying, "Glory to God in the highest!" or, "Peace on earth, goodwill to men!" or, "Christmas is Jesus' birthday.")

Order of Service

CHRISTMAS EVE

Introduction: This is the silent and holy night. It has now come. We have waited long and our excitement has grown with each passing day. We don't know if this is the exact day on which Christ was born. It really doesn't matter. We are not marking a date; we are noting a fact of fantastic proportions. We are rejoicing that God's Son, our Savior-King, did come. Now, as a family, let us have our final, pre-Christmas devotion. With it we bring Advent to a close for this year and open the door to Christmas itself.

Invocation: In the name of the Father and of the Son and of the Holy Ghost. Amen.

Prayer: O holy Child of Bethlehem,
Descend to us, we pray;
Cast out our sin And enter in,
Be born in us today.
We hear the Christmas angels
The great glad tidings tell.
Oh, come to us, Abide with us,
Our Lord, Immanuel!

Scripture: Luke 2:1-20

And it came to pass in those days that there went out a decree from Caesar Augustus that all the world should be taxed. (And this taxing was first made when Cyrenius was governor of Syria.) And all went to be taxed, everyone into his own city. And Joseph also went up from Galilee, out of the city of Nazareth, into Judea, unto the city of David, which is called Bethlehem (because he was of the house and lineage of David), to be taxed with Mary, his espoused wife, being great with child. And so it was that, while they were there, the days were accomplished that she should be delivered. And she brought forth her firstborn Son and wrapped Him in swaddling clothes and laid Him in a manger because there was no room for them in the inn.

And there were in the same country shepherds abiding in the field, keeping watch over their flock by night. And lo, the angel of the Lord came upon them, and the glory of the Lord shone round about them; and they were sore afraid. And the angel said unto them, Fear not, for behold, I bring you good tidings of great joy, which shall be to all people. For unto you is born this day in the city of David a Savior, which is Christ the Lord. And this shall be a sign unto you: ye shall find the Babe wrapped in swaddling clothes, lying in a manger. And suddenly there was with the angel a multitude of the heavenly host praising God and saying, Glory to God in the highest, and on earth peace, goodwill toward men.

And it came to pass, as the angels were gone away from them into heaven, the shepherds said one to another, Let us now go even unto Bethlehem and see this thing which is come to pass, which the Lord hath made known unto us. And they came with haste and found Mary and Joseph, and the Babe lying in a manger. And when they had seen it, they made known abroad the saying which was told them concerning this Child. And all they that heard it wondered at those things which were told them by the shepherds. But Mary kept all these things and pondered them in her heart. And the shepherds returned, glorifying and praising God for all the things that they had heard and seen, as it was told unto them.

Sentence Prayers: (*Let each member of the family in his own words express his Christmas joy and thankfulness through a brief prayer.*)

Hymn: Silent Night! Holy Night!

Closing Prayer: May the preparation we have made for this Christmas glorify You, O God. May it bring to us true peace and happiness. Let the spirit of our Christmas celebration be with us all year, and by it guide us to a greater faith and a surer trust in You. This we ask in Jesus' name. Amen.

The Incarnation

CHRISTMAS DAY

Galatians 4:4, 5

This is the day, the day we have waited for so long. If it has seemed a long time for us, think of the children of the Old Testament who for years and years looked forward to the first Christmas. When the day finally came, one grand, old man of faith, Simeon, looked at the baby Jesus and prayed: "Lord, now lettest Thou Thy servant depart in peace according to Thy word; for mine eyes have seen Thy Salvation, which Thou hast prepared before the face of all people, a Light to lighten the Gentiles and the Glory of Thy people Israel" (Luke 2:29-32). For to what did Isaiah, Jeremiah, and the thousands of faithful in the Old Testament look forward? What happened that made Simeon ready to die but to die happy? In one word, the answer is the Incarnation.

That's a big word. It ought to be, for it cloaks a big thought. Incarnation means, literally, "made into flesh." To Christians its full meaning is this: God came down from the heights of heaven and became a man like us, in order that He might overcome our sins for us. The Incarnation is the doorway by which Christ entered this life. The Resurrection and the Ascension are the doorways by which He left. Each one of these words describes something that Christ did for us. He became a human being for us; He rose from the dead for us; He ascended into heaven for us. Because He came into the flesh and lived as God's Child, we can live confidently as God's children. Because He conquered death and rose from the grave, we are confident of conquering death and rising from the grave. Because He finally ascended into heaven, we are confident that we shall ascend to heaven and there live eternally. All this started for us with the Incarnation.

More than that, we can be confident God knows us and knows our needs, for He walked our way and lived our life. Like us, He was born of a woman and born under the Law. He became man in every sense of the word. But as a man He overcame our restrictions and burst the chains of sin and Satan, not only for Himself but also for us.

That's some of what this day we call Christmas means. It is the remembrance of God's greater answer to man's very great need. In terms of human history it all began with the coming of Christ as a baby in Bethlehem. Each year we remember this great event again, for it was the beginning of 33 earth-shaking years, 33 life-saving years, 33 heaven-opening years. Christmas marks the Incarnation. When you know that, then you can have a merry Christmas. Since you do know, make this Christmas merry by remembering it and rejoicing in it.

A Child Is Born
in Bethlehem

A Child is born in Bethlehem, in Bethlehem.
Great joy then in Jerusalem! Alleluia! Alleluia!

A humble maiden sat alone, she sat alone.
The King of heaven sent down His own. Alleluia! Alleluia!

The manger held the blessed Boy, the blessed Boy.
God's angels sang a song of joy. Alleluia! Alleluia!

Eternal thanks and praise we bring, all praise we bring,
And to the Holy Three we sing. Alleluia! Alleluia!

Anonymous 14th-century Danish hymn

All Glory for
This Blessed Morn

From east to west, from shore to shore
Let every heart awake and sing
The holy Child whom Mary bore,
The Christ, the everlasting King.

He shrank not from the oxen's stall,
He lay within the manger bed,
And He, whose bounty feedeth all,
At Mary's breast Himself was fed.

And while the angels in the sky
Sang praise above the silent field,
To shepherds poor the Lord most high,
The one great Shepherd, was revealed.

All glory for this blessed morn
To God the Father ever be,
All praise to Thee, O Virgin-born,
All praise, O Holy Ghost, to Thee.

Coelius Sedulius (died ca. 450)

O Lord, How Shall
I Meet Thee

O Lord, how shall I meet Thee,
How welcome Thee aright?
Thy people long to greet Thee,
My Hope, my heart's Delight!
Oh, kindle, Lord most holy,
Thy lamp within my breast
To do in spirit lowly
All that may please Thee best.

Love caused Thy incarnation,
Love brought Thee down to me;
Thy thirst for my salvation
Procured my liberty.
O love beyond all telling,
That led Thee to embrace,
In love all love excelling,
Our lost and fallen race!

Rejoice, then, ye sad-hearted,
Who sit in deepest gloom,
Who mourn o'er joys departed
And tremble at your doom.
Despair not, He is near you,
Yea, standing at the door,
Who best can help and cheer you
And bids you weep no more.

Paul Gerhardt

HERE COMES CHRISTMAS

A CHRISTMAS CRÉCHE

MATERIALS TO BE USED

Light cardboard — for manger and adult bodies
3 plastic foam balls or Christmas tree ornaments (2 large, 1 small)
Gift-wrap aluminum foil — to cover bodies
Colored construction paper — for arms of Mary and Joseph
Glue
Scissors
Felt — for beard and Joseph's shawl
Pipe Cleaner
Ribbon — for Joseph's sash
Yarn — about 100 feet (40' for Mary's hair, 40' for manger hay, plus a little for Baby's hair)
Tape — to reinforce manger
White paper — for Baby's body and arms

The figures above are a delightful way to show and express the Christmas story. Each figure is constructed in the same basic way by using paper cones for the bodies and plastic foam balls for the heads.

JOSEPH — Cut a circle, with a radius of 7 inches, from a sheet of fairly heavy paper. Cut the circle in half and use one half for Joseph's body and save the other half for Mary's body. Fold the semicircle into a cone and glue it closed. Now cut a semicircle, with a radius of 8 inches, from gift-wrap foil; wrap this around the paper cone and tuck the ends up into the bottom (see Figure 1). Using pattern piece 1, cut out Joseph's arms from colored construction paper. Attach them on the back of the cone about an inch from the top (see Figure 2). Glue the right hand to the front of Joseph's body as shown in the diagram. To attach the head to the body take the pointed end of a pencil and poke a hole in the plastic foam ball. Put a few drops of glue into the hole, and place the pointed end of the cone into the hole. Let this dry a few minutes while cutting out Joseph's shawl (piece 6) and his beard (piece 5) from the felt. Glue the beard and shawl to his head. In order to keep the shawl close to Joseph's head, wrap a pipe cleaner around the shawl and head (see Figure 3). Cut his eyes from shiny paper and glue them on. Color in his mouth with red paint or ink. For his sash, tie a piece of ribbon around the waist.

MARY — Use the semicircle remaining from Joseph for Mary's body. Cut an inch off the rounded part, making a radius of 6 inches instead of 7 inches. Fold the semicircle into a cone. Since Mary is to be in a kneeling position, measure ¾ inch up from the bottom of the front of the cone (see Figure 4). From the center front at the ¾ inch mark, cut halfway around one side of the cone, tapering it to nothing in the back of the cone. Do the same thing for the other side (see Figure 4). Cut a semicircle with a radius of 7 inches from gift-wrap foil. Wrap it around the cone as before (see Figure 1). Attach Mary's arms in the back, bringing her hands together in the front and gluing them as though in prayer. Attach the head in the same way as Joseph's was done. For her hair, cut about forty 12-inch strips of yarn. Tie them together in the center (see Figure 5). Glue the hair onto the head with the center close to her

41

forehead (see Figure 6). Sweep the yarn towards the back and trim. Cut her eyes and mouth from paper and glue them onto her face.

MANGER — Pattern piece 7 is the manger. Cut it out of heavy paper and fold it according to the fold lines shown on the pattern. Reinforce the legs with tape (see Figure 7).

The hay for the manger is made from 40 pieces of yarn about 12 inches long (see Figure 5). Place it in the manger and spread the ends over the sides.

BABY — Cut the Baby's body and arms from white paper, using pattern pieces 3 and 4. Fold the body into a cone and attach the arms and head in the same way as the adult figures. Cut small pieces of yarn for His hair and glue it onto His head. Cut His eyes and mouth from paper and glue them onto His face.

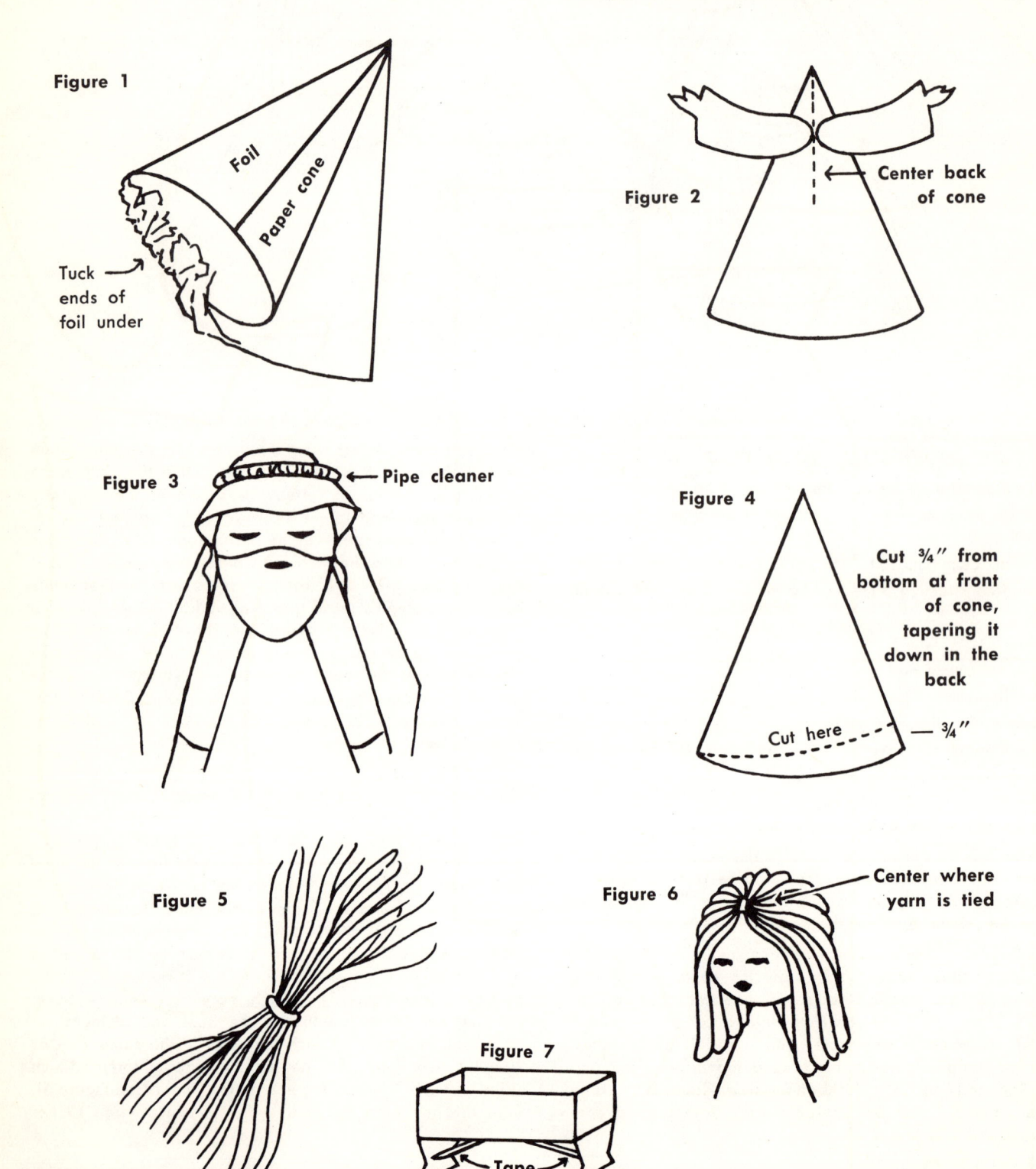

Figure 1 — Foil, Paper cone, Tuck ends of foil under

Figure 2 — Center back of cone

Figure 3 — Pipe cleaner

Figure 4 — Cut ¾" from bottom at front of cone, tapering it down in the back. Cut here — ¾"

Figure 5

Figure 6 — Center where yarn is tied

Figure 7 — Tape

3

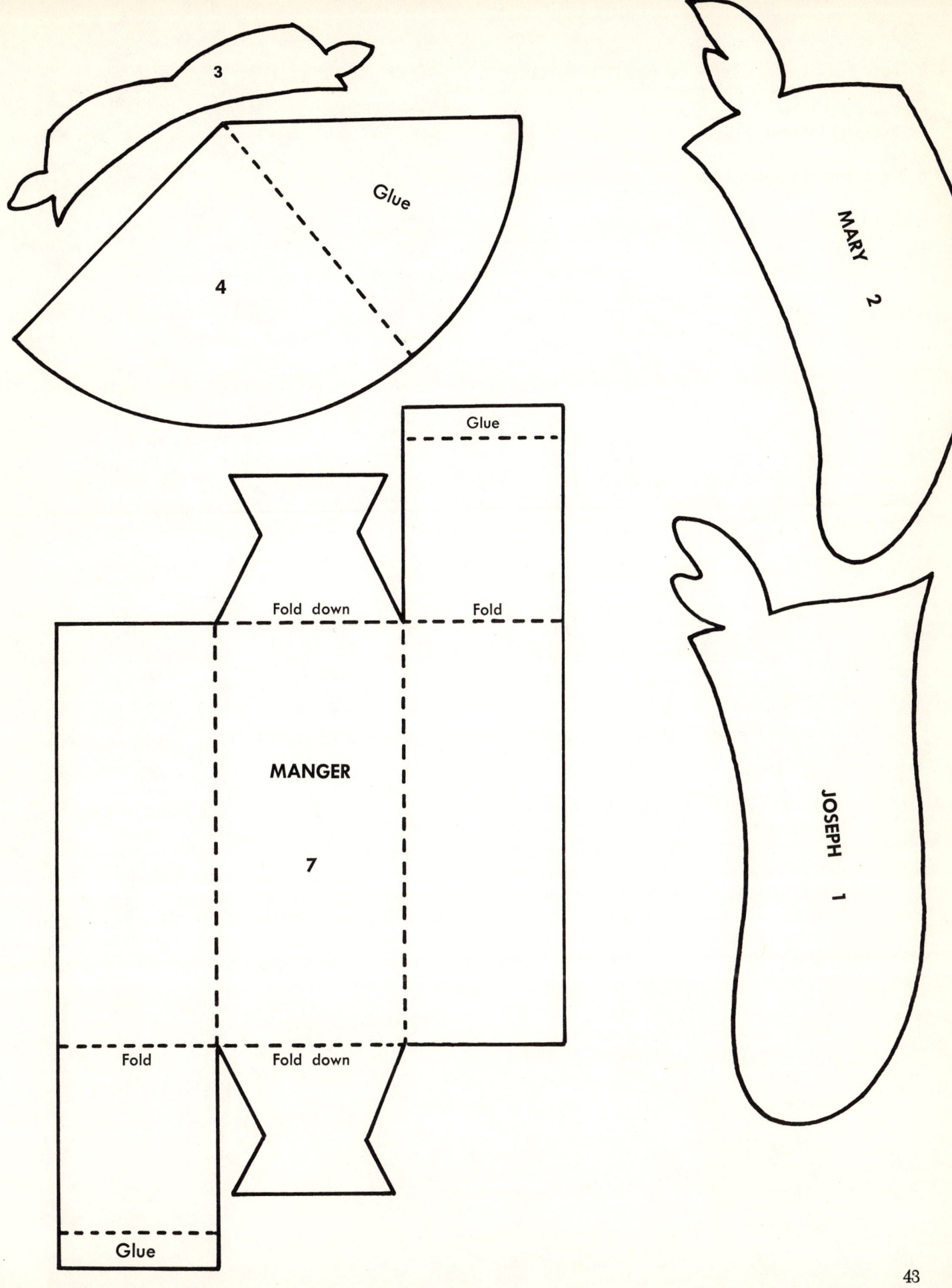

Glue

4

Glue

Fold down | Fold

MANGER

7

Fold | Fold down

Glue

MARY 2

JOSEPH 1

43

⌒ — Baby's eye
‿ — Baby's mouth

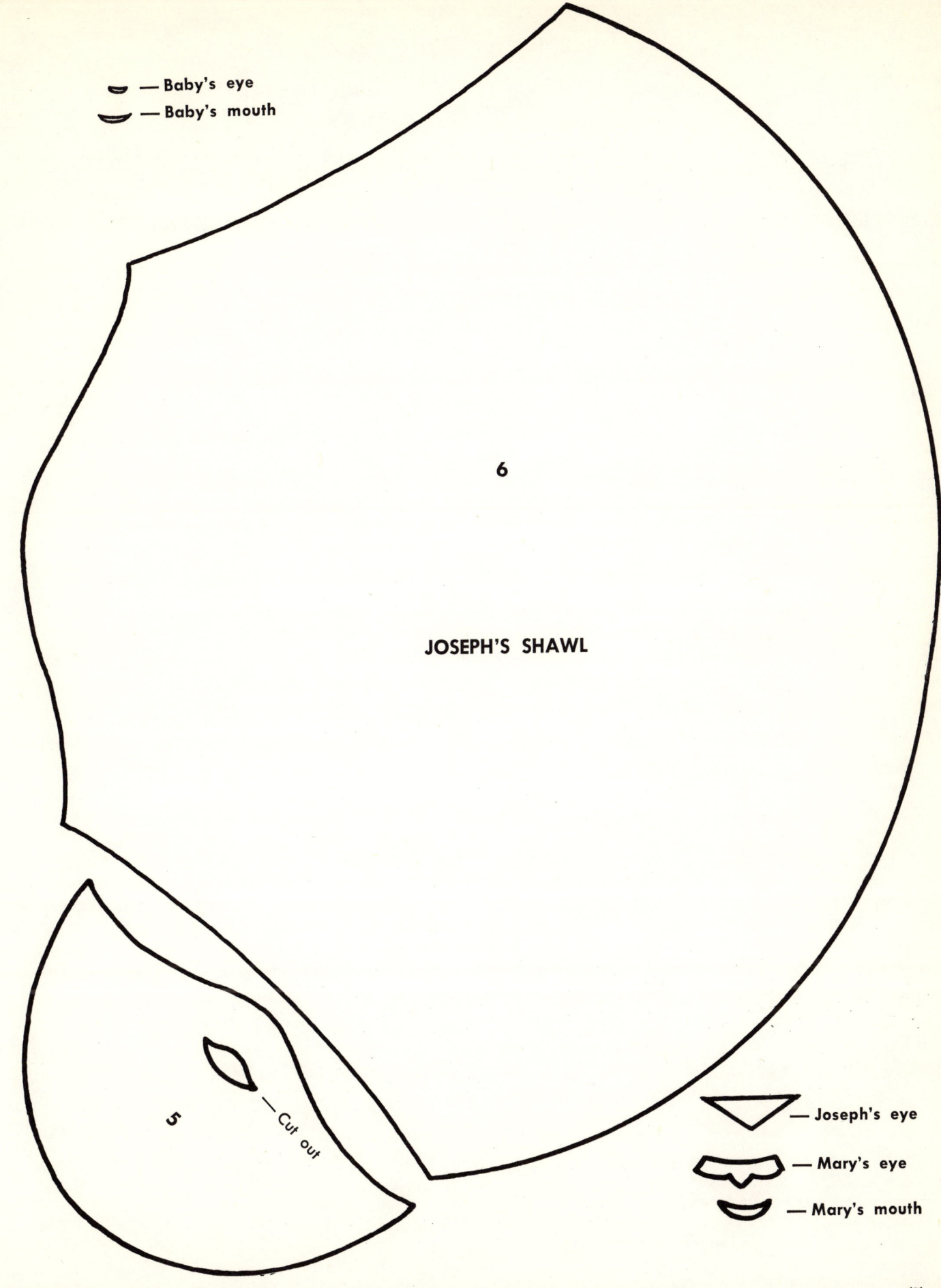

6

JOSEPH'S SHAWL

5

— Cut out

▽ — Joseph's eye
— Mary's eye
‿ — Mary's mouth

45

HERE COMES CHRISTMAS

A CHRISTIAN CHRISTMAS TREE BASE

MATERIALS NEEDED:

Glue

Scissors

Felt (white, 54" square; red, 11" × 8"; green, 8" × 14"; yellow, 7" × 17"; light blue, 5" × 9"; brown, 13" × 20"; pink, 8" × 8"; black, 3" × 5"; dark blue, 9" × 14")

1. CUTTING OUT THE PIECES: Cut a circle with a diameter of about 1½ yards. From a point on the outer edge of the circle cut a straight line to the center of the circle. From the center cut a circle 5 or 6 inches in diameter. Cut out each individual piece from the correct color of felt, using the "Pattern Layout Directions" as a guide.

2. ASSEMBLING THE FIGURES: Basically, all of the figures are assembled in the same way. The guide sheet will show how and where each piece is to be placed.

3. THE ROBES: Take the bottom parts of the robes (pieces 6, 17, 22, 34). Following the guide sheet, glue the top parts of the robes (pieces 10, 13, 16, 21, 28, 33, 37) onto the correct bottom parts.

4. HEADS (Pieces 2, 4, 23, 30): Mary, Wise Man I, Shepherd I, and Shepherd II heads are glued onto top parts of robes or hats. In the case of Wise Men II and III the heads are glued to shoulders. (See sketch)

5. BEARDS: Glue the beards (pieces 3, 12, 31, 5) onto the heads of the men figures. The hair and beard of Wise Man II is all one piece, but it is still glued onto the head in the same way.

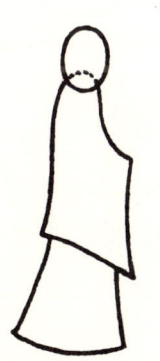

WISE MAN II
WISE MAN III

MARY, WISE MAN I
SHEPHERD I
SHEPHERD II

6. HATS (Pieces 8, 11, 15, 35, 38): Glue the hats directly onto the heads of the figures.

7. HALOS: Mary and Joseph have halos (piece 7). Glue them onto the backs of their heads.

8. HANDS (Piece 1): Glue the wrist part of the hand onto the sleeve of the figures.

9. EYES (Piece 40): Glue the eyes onto the faces of the figures.

10. REMAINING PARTS OF THE FIGURES: The Wise Men's gifts (pieces 9, 14, and 18) and the shepherd's staff are the remaining parts. Glue them onto the correct figures.

11. COMPLETING THE FIGURES: Indicate the folds in the robes by outlining them with a pen or pencil.

12. MANGER: Glue the hay (pieces 25, 26) onto the manger (piece 24). The guide sheet shows the exact placement. Next, glue the Baby (piece 29) onto the back of the manger so it looks as if He is sitting. Glue the Baby's halo (piece 27) onto the back of His head.

13. STABLE: Glue the top part (piece 19) onto the posts (piece 20).

14. SHEEP: The only thing to be done to the sheep is to outline them with a pen or pencil so they will be visible when placed on the background.

15. PLACING THE ITEMS ON THE CIRCLE: Glue all of the figures onto the circle, according to the guide sheet, placing them about 4 inches from the outer edge of the circle. Make sure that the center of the stable is directly opposite the line that was cut in the back of the circle.

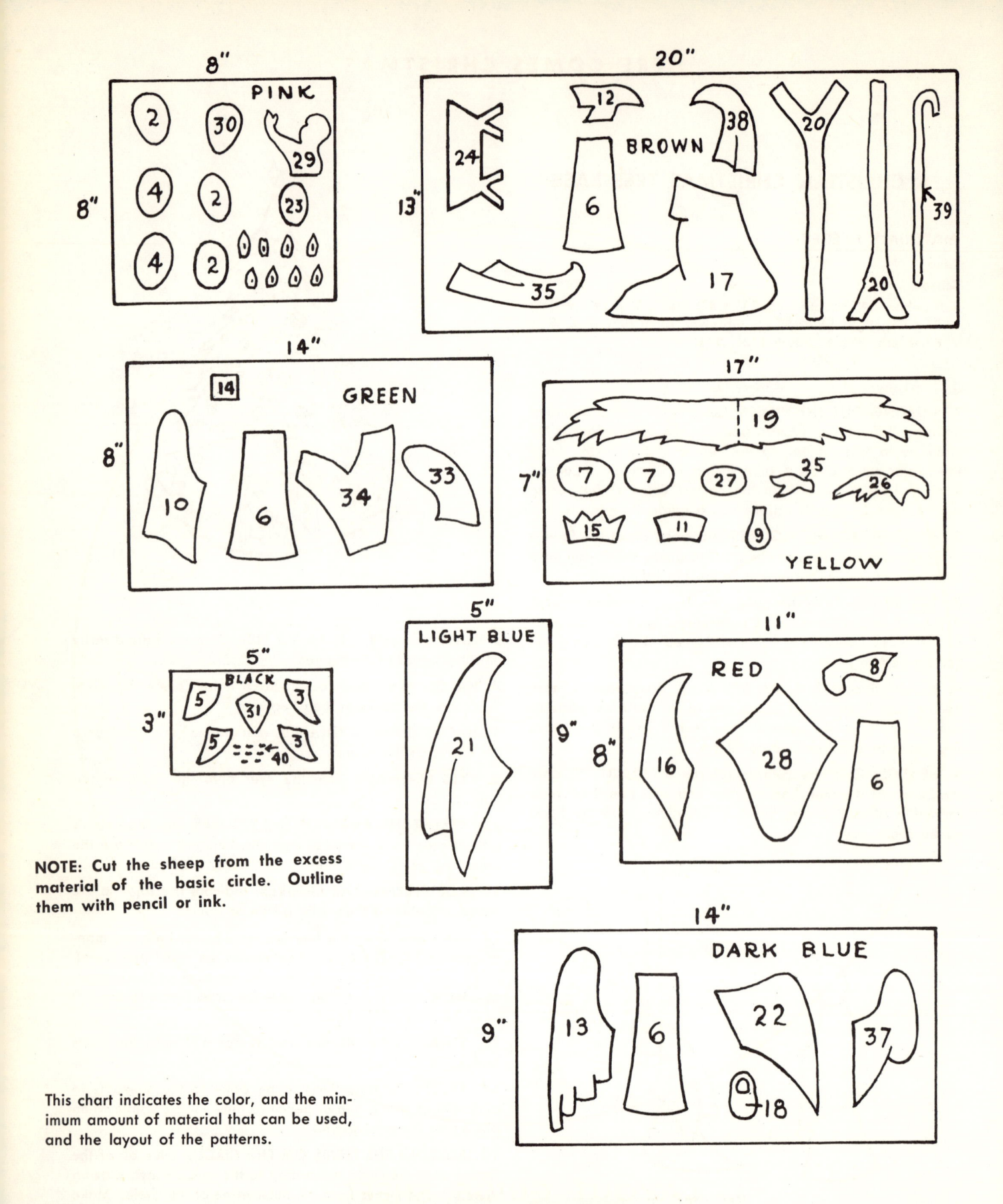

NOTE: Cut the sheep from the excess material of the basic circle. Outline them with pencil or ink.

This chart indicates the color, and the minimum amount of material that can be used, and the layout of the patterns.

PATTERN LAYOUT DIRECTIONS

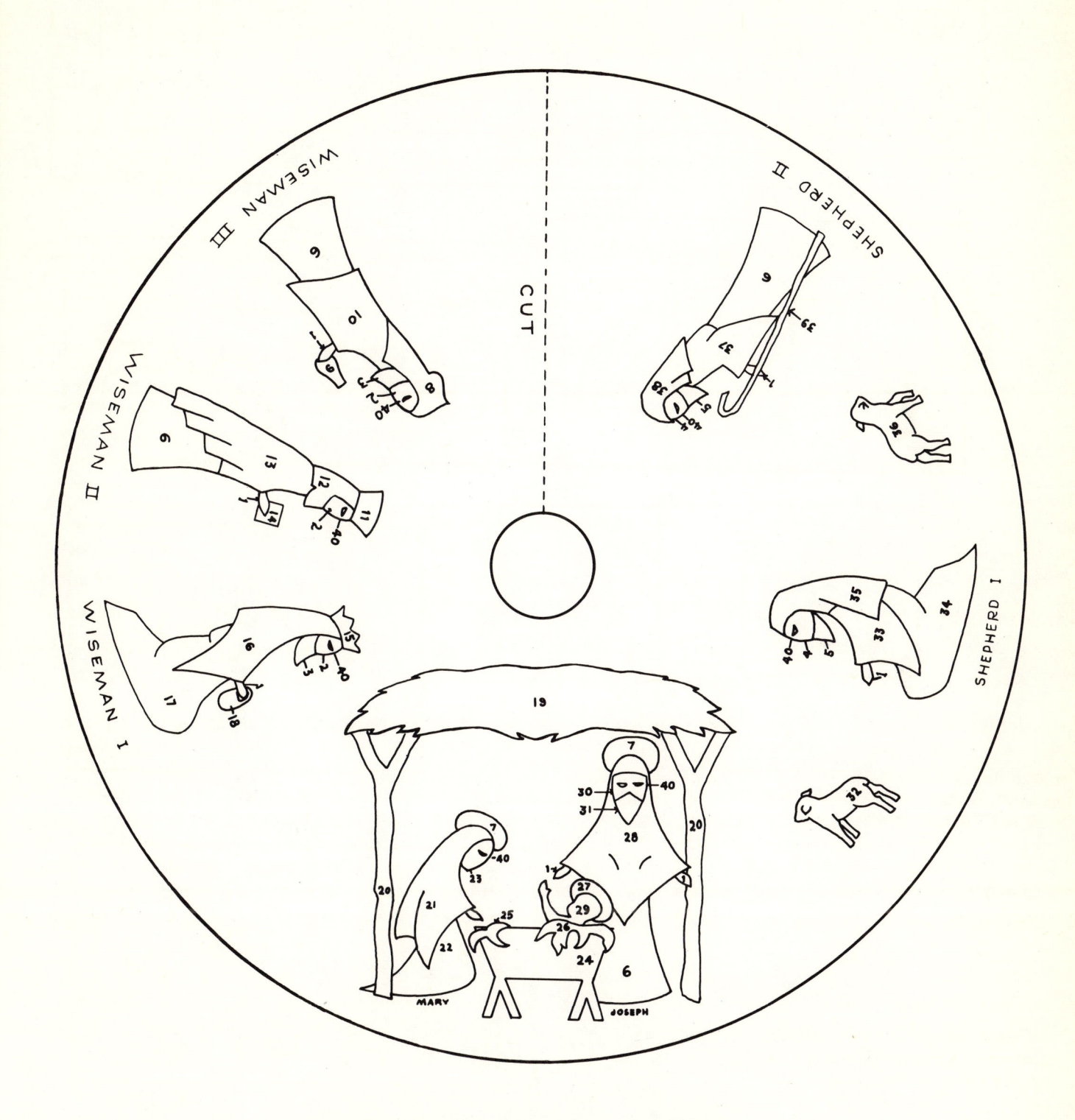

LAYOUT GUIDE SHEET

51

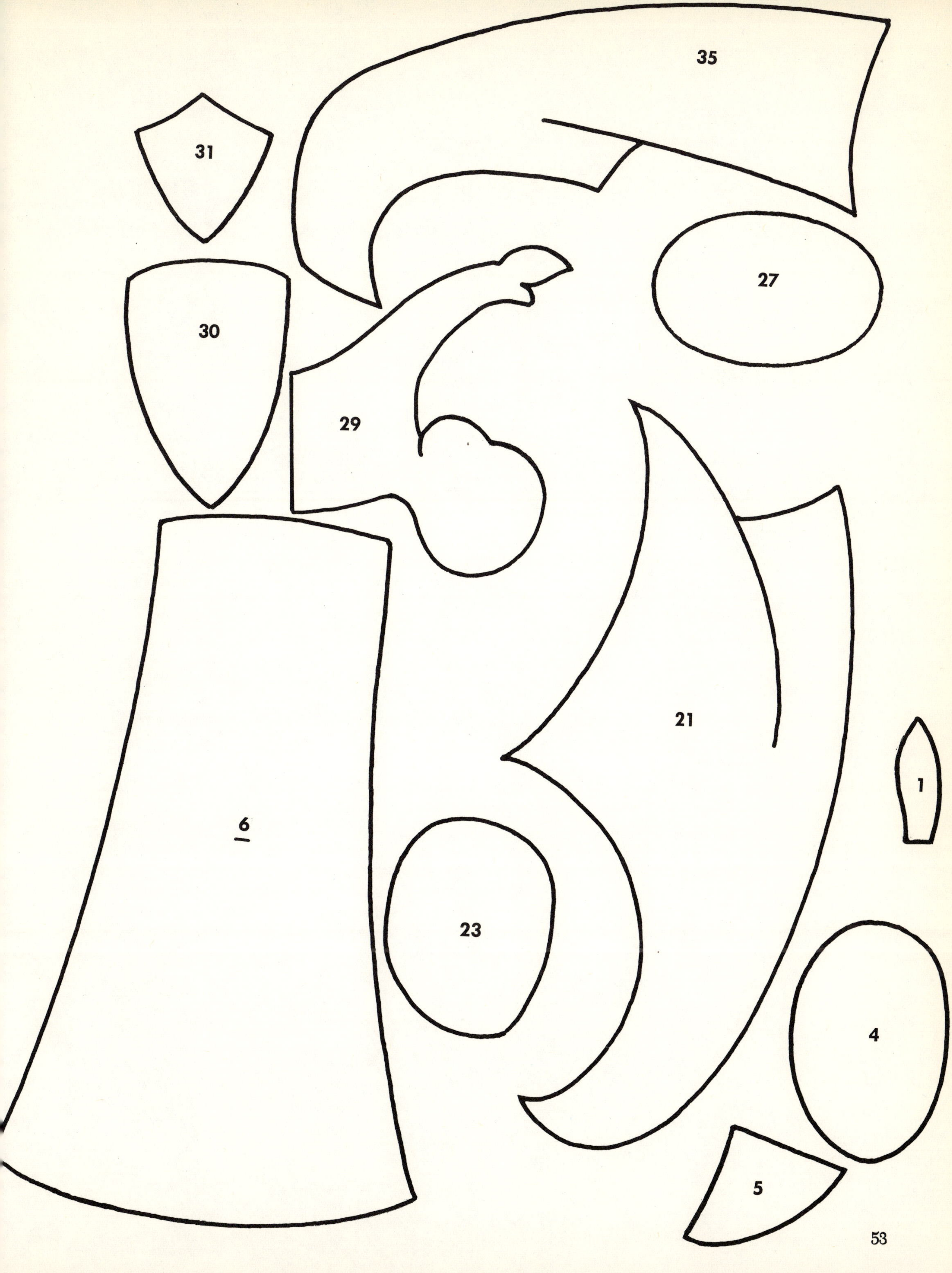
35
31
27
30
29
21
1
6
23
4
5

20

36

8

19
(Double This Piece)

26

25

FOLD

55

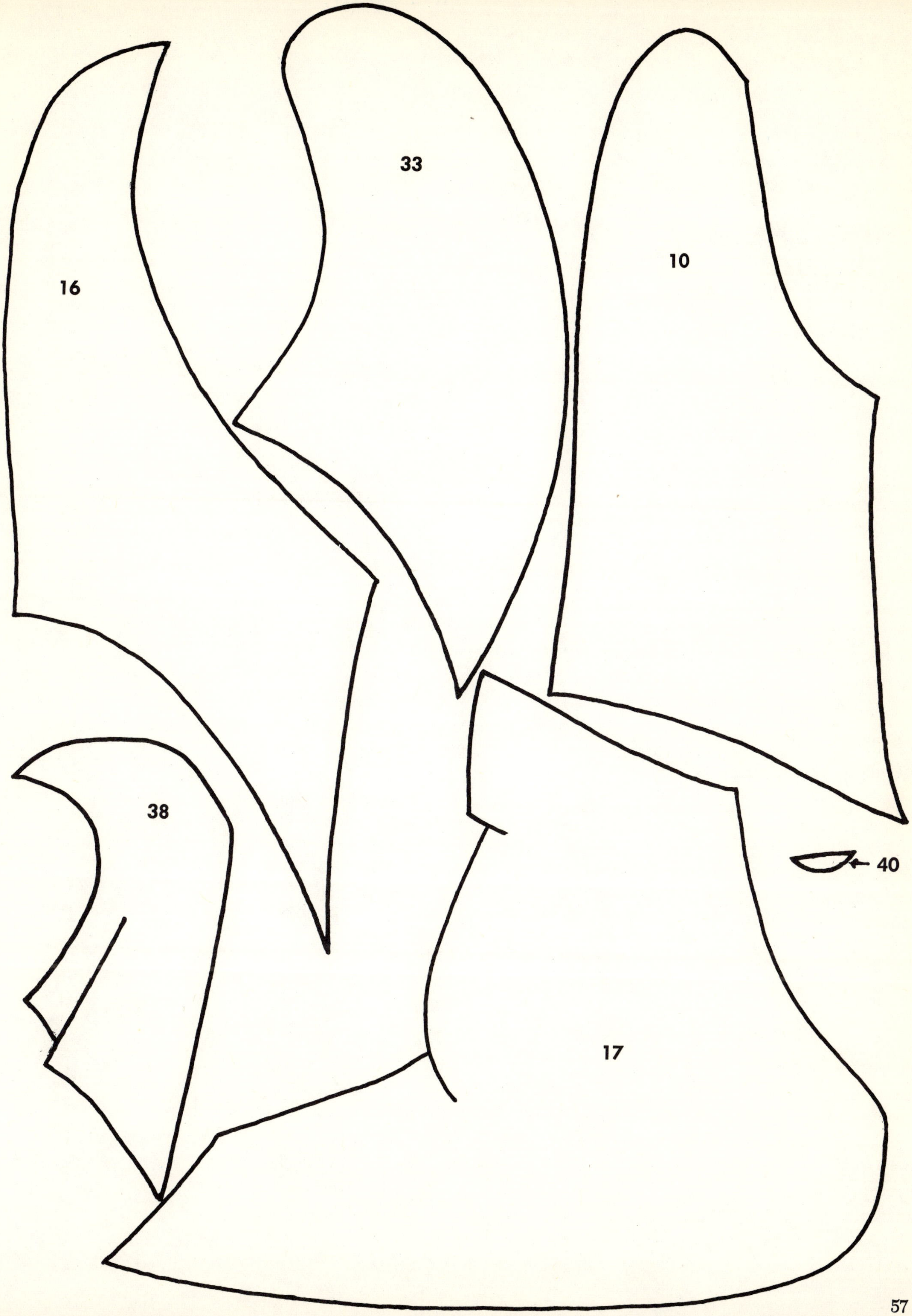

33
10
16
38
40
17

39 12 2 13 28 3 22

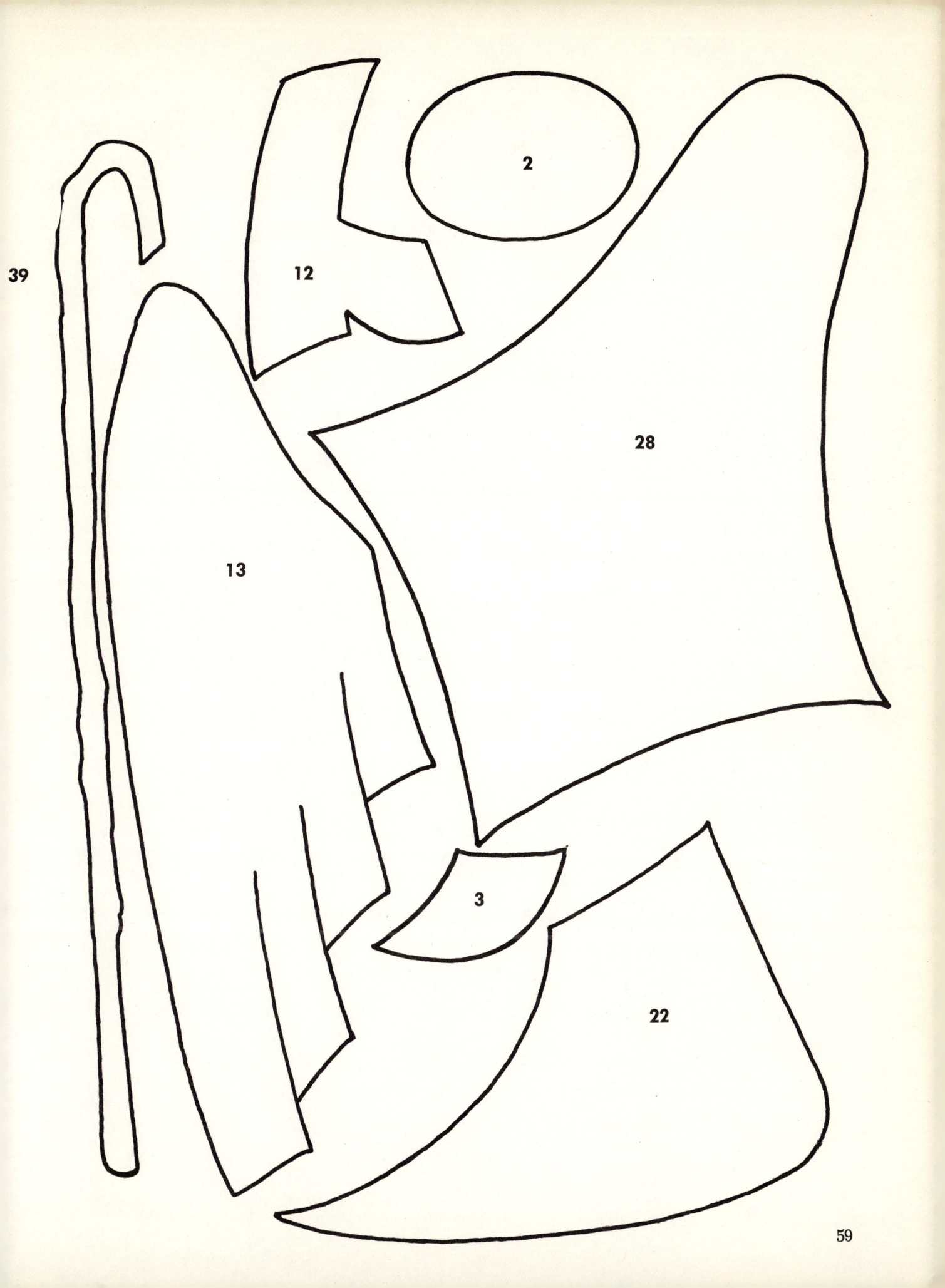

59

"Hark the Glad Sound! The Savior Comes"

1. Hark the glad sound! The Savior comes,
   The Savior promised long;
   Let every heart prepare a throne
   And every voice a song.

2. He comes the prisoners to release,
   In Satan's bondage held.
   The gates of brass before Him burst,
   The iron fetters yield.

3. He comes the broken heart to bind,
   The bleeding soul to cure,
   And with the treasures of His grace
   T'enrich the humble poor.

4. Our glad hosannas, Prince of Peace,
   Thy welcome shall proclaim
   And heaven's eternal arches ring
   With Thy belovèd name.

"Lift Up Your Heads, Ye Mighty Gates"

1. Lift up your heads, ye mighty gates!
   Behold, the King of Glory waits;
   The King of kings is drawing near,
   The Savior of the world is here.
   Life and salvation He doth bring,
   Wherefore rejoice and gladly sing:
   We praise Thee, Father, now,
   Creator, wise art Thou!

2. A Helper just He comes to thee,
   His chariot is humility,
   His kingly crown is holiness,
   His scepter, pity in distress.
   The end of all our woe He brings;
   Wherefore the earth is glad and sings:
   We praise Thee, Savior, now,
   Mighty in deed art Thou!

3. Fling wide the portals of your heart;
   Make it a temple set apart
   From earthly use for Heaven's employ,
   Adorned with prayer and love and joy.
   So shall your Sovereign enter in
   And new and nobler life begin.
   To Thee, O God, be praise
   For Word and deed and grace!

4. Redeemer, come! I open wide
   My heart to Thee; here, Lord, abide!
   Let me Thine inner presence feel,
   Thy grace and love in me reveal;
   Thy Holy Spirit guide us on
   Until our glorious goal is won.
   Eternal praise and fame
   We offer to Thy name.

"On Jordan's Bank the Baptist's Cry"

1. On Jordan's bank the Baptist's cry
   Announces that the Lord is nigh;
   Come, then, and hearken, for he brings
   Glad tidings from the King of kings.

2. Then cleansed be every Christian breast
   And furnished for so great a Guest.
   Yea, let us each our hearts prepare
   For Christ to come and enter there.

3. For Thou art our Salvation, Lord,
   Our Refuge, and our great Reward.
   Without Thy grace our souls must fade
   And wither like a flower decayed.

4. All praise, eternal Son, to Thee
   Whose advent sets Thy people free,
   Whom, with the Father, we adore
   And Holy Ghost forevermore.

"Oh, Come, Oh, Come, Emmanuel"

1. Oh, come, oh, come, Emmanuel,
   And ransom captive Israel
   That mourns in lonely exile here
   Until the Son of God appear.
   Rejoice! Rejoice! Emmanuel
   Shall come to thee, O Israel.

2. Oh, come, Thou Rod of Jesse, free
   Thine own from Satan's tyranny;
   From depths of hell Thy people save
   And give them victory o'er the grave.
   Rejoice! Rejoice! Emmanuel
   Shall come to thee, O Israel.

3. Oh, come, Thou Dayspring from on high,
   And cheer us by Thy drawing nigh;
   Disperse the gloomy clouds of night
   And death's dark shadows put to flight.
   Rejoice! Rejoice! Emmanuel
   Shall come to thee, O Israel.

4. Oh, come, Thou Key of David, come
   And open wide our heavenly home;
   Make safe the way that leads on high
   And close the path to misery.
   Rejoice! Rejoice! Emmanuel
   Shall come to thee, O Israel.